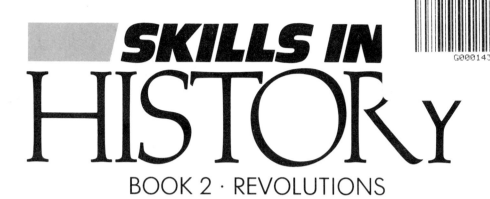

SKILLS IN
HISTORY
BOOK 2 · REVOLUTIONS

Heinemann Educational,
a division of Heinemann Educational Books Ltd,
Halley Court, Jordan Hill, Oxford OX2 8EJ

OXFORD LONDON EDINBURGH
MELBOURNE SYDNEY AUCKLAND
IBADAN NAIROBI GABORONE HARARE
KINGSTON PORTSMOUTH NH (USA)
SINGAPORE MADRID

First published 1989
Reprinted 1989, 1990

British Library Cataloguing in Publication Data

Shuter, Paul
    Skills in history.
    Bk. 2: Revolutions
    1. History
    I. Title   II. Child, John, 1951–900

    ISBN 0 435 31863 2

Printed in Great Britain by Scotprint, Edinburgh

ISBN 0 435 31866 7
(Teacher's Set)

Cover photograph: By permission of the Earl of Rosebery

Other titles in the *Skills in History* series:

Book 1 Changes
An introductory section explains what chronology is,
how historians work, the clues they look for, the
differences between primary and secondary sources and
how they are used. There are further sections on the
Romans, Saxons, Normans and Tudors.

Book 3 The Twentieth Century
Focusing on modern world history, this book includes
double-page spreads on the First World War; the Russian
revolution and Stalin; the USA during the 1920s and
1930s; the General Strike in Britain; Mussolini; the
Weimar Republic and Hitler's Germany; the Spanish
Civil War; the Second World War; the Cold War; China;
Vietnam; the Middle East; Africa; India; and much more.

SKILLS IN
HISTORY

BOOK 2 · REVOLUTIONS

Series Editor: PAUL SHUTER

PAUL SHUTER   JOHN CHILD   DAVID TAYLOR

HEINEMANN
EDUCATIONAL

Contents

Death of a Queen

In the early months of 1603 **Queen Elizabeth I** was an old, sick, and lonely woman. Almost all the courtiers of her own age were dead. The men who had been her chief advisers throughout her reign were dead. Elizabeth had refused to say who should rule England after her death. The obvious choice was **James VI of Scotland**, but there were other possible candidates.

During March Elizabeth's health got dramatically worse. She refused to go to her bed and sat in a chair day and night. She refused food. She also refused to be treated by her doctors. One courtier, Sir Robert Carey, planned carefully what to do when she died. He arranged for a string of fast horses to be waiting at intervals between Richmond, where Elizabeth was dying, and Edinburgh, where James VI was waiting for news. He hoped that if he were the first to tell James he would be well rewarded.

The **Privy Council**, Elizabeth's chief ministers, ordered that nobody should travel to Scotland. On the night of 23–24 March, Carey waited in the gatehouse of Richmond Palace for a signal that Elizabeth had died. Between 2 and 3 o'clock the signal was given, and Carey began his ride. He arrived in Edinburgh late on 26 March and was the first to tell James of Elizabeth's death. Meanwhile, on 24 March, in London the Privy Council had proclaimed James the new King of England, **James I**.

The succession

The way the crown was passed between one monarch and the next in England was usually quite simple. The crown went to the eldest son of the previous ruler. If there were no living sons, then it went to the eldest daughter. If the previous ruler had no living children at all, then the crown went to the eldest brother or his children. If there were no brothers, it went to the eldest sister and her children. If the dead ruler had no living brothers or sisters, then the crown went to uncles and aunts, then great uncles and great-aunts and so on.

Elizabeth's father, Henry VIII, had been succeeded by his eldest son, Edward VI. This happened even though Edward was not Henry's eldest child. Edward had no brothers, so he was succeeded by Mary I, his elder sister. When Mary died childless, Elizabeth I, her sister, became the next queen. When Elizabeth died childless all the children of Henry VIII were dead, and none of them had had children of their own. The next monarch would be found by going back to Henry VII's children.

Source A

'My throne has been the throne of kings: neither ought any other than my next heir succeed me.'

Elizabeth, in January 1603, when asked who should be the next ruler of England.

Source B

'I have said that my throne was the throne of kings, and that I would not that any base [low-born person] should succeed me.'

And when she was asked what this meant: 'I will that a King succeed me, and who but my kinsman the King of Scots.'

Elizabeth, when asked by her Privy Council who should succeed her, during her last illness in March 1603.

Rulers of England, 1603–1702	
James I	1603–25
Charles I	1625–49
The Commonwealth	1649–53
The Protectorate	1653–9
The Commonwealth	1659–60
Charles II	1660–85
James II	1685–8
William III and Mary II	1688–1702

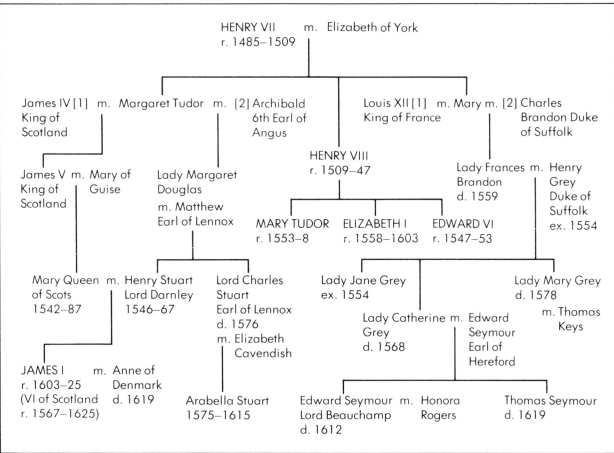

Descendants of Henry VII.

Questions

Section A

1 What plan did Sir Robert Carey make for when Elizabeth died?

2 a What would the Privy Council have thought of Carey's plan?
  b Why do you think Carey set up his plan?

3 What happened when Elizabeth died?

Section B

4 Write out the following lists of events in **chronological order** (that is, the order in which they happened).

  a James becoming King of Scotland; Elizabeth becoming Queen; James becoming King of England; Elizabeth dying.
  b Carey arranging for horses on the road to Scotland; Elizabeth falling ill; James coming to England; Elizabeth dying.

5 Draw a time-line of the years 1603 to 1702. Mark on it the reigns of each of the different rulers.

6 Draw a time-line covering the years from AD 42 to now.

  a Mark on it the years covered by the rulers on your last time-line.
  b Mark on your own life so far.
  c Find out when the following events happened and mark them on: The Battle of Hastings; King John signing Magna Carta; Henry VII becoming King of England; the defeat of the Spanish Armada; the opening of the Liverpool-to-Manchester Railway; the reign of Queen Victoria; the First World War; the Second World War.

King James VI and I

James I did not have an easy childhood. Soon after James's birth, his mother, **Mary Queen of Scots**, was thought to have been involved in the murder of his father. The Scots nobles rose up against her and her new lover, Bothwell. In 1567 Mary, who was imprisoned by the nobles, abdicated in favour of James. He was thirteen months old. The next year she escaped and fled to England. James never saw her again.

While James was too young to rule, Scotland was ruled by a **regent** (a noble who used most of the King's powers). Groups of nobles competed for power. One regent was executed, and for a time James was kidnapped by a group who did not like the way the country was governed.

When James became King of England he was 37. He had been a success in Scotland and had done much to bring the country to peace. He came to England with strong ideas about the powers kings should have but with very little money. Compared to England, Scotland was poor.

On his slow journey from Scotland to London in 1603 James was welcomed by crowds at every town. Many things happened on his journey which were warnings for the rest of his reign. He never seemed to have enough money, and he had to send to the Privy Council in London for money and jewels for his journey. He did not always understand the customs of his new country. When a pickpocket was caught in the crowd which welcomed the King in Newark, James ordered that he should be hanged at once. After the pickpocket had been hanged, James's councillors quietly explained that in England the King did not have the power to put anyone to death without trial.

Source A

Part of a speech made by James I to Parliament on 21 March 1610

'Kings are not only God's lieutenants on earth, but even by God himself they are called gods. If you will consider the powers of God, you shall see how they agree with those of a king. God has power to create or destroy, make or unmake, at his pleasure. To give life or send death, to judge all and be judged by none. To raise low things and make high things low at his pleasure. And the like power have kings. They make and unmake their subjects. They have power of raising, and casting down; of life and of death, judges over all their subjects. Yet they may be judged by none but God only. They make of their subjects like men at chess – a pawn to take a bishop or a knight.'

Source B

'Three qualities of the mind he possesses: he understands clearly, judges wisely, and has a good memory. In any argument, whatever it is about, he maintains the view that appears to him most just. He is timid, yet he has a great desire to be thought brave; there is nothing he will not try for the sake of his reputation. Having heard that a Scottish lord went two days and two nights without sleep, the King went three.'

Monsieur Fontenay, writing to Mary Queen of Scots, 15 August 1584. Mary had sent Fontenay to try to persuade James to help her. Fontenay couldn't persuade James to help, but he sent Mary back this description of her son, who she had not seen for seventeen years.

Source C

'He was of middle height, more fat because of his clothes than in his body. His clothes always being made large and easy, the doublets quilted to be dagger proof, his breeches in great pleats and full stuffed. He was naturally of a timorous disposition, which was the reason for his quilted doublets. His eyes large, ever rolling after any stranger that came into his presence. His beard was very thin. His tongue too large for his mouth, which made him drink very badly, as if eating his drink, which came out into the cup of each side of his mouth. His skin was soft because he never washed his hands, only rubbed his finger ends slightly with the wet end of a napkin.'

Sir Anthony Weldon, writing about James after 1617. Weldon had been employed in James's court, but he lost his job in 1617 when an anti-Scots pamphlet he wrote was discovered.

For the rest of his reign James continued to spend far too much money. Many of his problems with **Parliament** were caused by money. He was especially generous to courtiers who became his favourites. This upset many people even more; people thought the taxes were too high, didn't approve of the favourites and then saw much of the King's money given away.

Source D

'I have noticed in him three faults. He does not realise his poverty and lack of power. Instead he is over-confident of his strength and scornful of other princes. His love of favourites is not wise, and takes no account of the wishes of his people. He is too lazy about affairs, too given to pleasure, allowing all business to be conducted by others.'

Source E

'He was very witty, and had as many witty jests as any man living. He would not smile himself at these, but deliver them in a grave and serious manner. He spent much, and had much use of his subjects' purses. This bred some clashes with them in Parliament, yet he would always come off in the end with a sweet and reasonable close.'

Source F

James VI and I.

Questions

Section A

1 What things happened to James in Scotland which may have influenced him for the rest of his life?

2 Why might people in England have objected to James' favourites?

3 What did James think about the powers of a king?

Section B

Historians always want to know *where, when* and *why* a source was made. This helps them decide whether to trust it or not.

4 a Does Source B give a kind, or an unkind, picture of James?
 b Where, when and why was Source B written?
 c Does this help you decide whether to trust Source B?

5 a Does Source C give a kind, or an unkind, picture of James?
 b Where, when and why was Source C written?
 c Does this help you decide whether to trust Source C?

6 a Does Source F agree or disagree with any of the parts of Sources B and C?
 b Where there are disagreements, is Source F more likely to be correct?

7 Why is it hard to decide whether to trust Sources D and E?

8 Sources D and E both come from the same sources as B and C. Which is which?

9 If you had to write about the character of James I, which sources would you use? Give reasons for your answer.

5

Religion

The **Church of England** was the biggest and the richest organisation in the seventeenth century. No business made as much money as the Church. No family owned as much land as the Church. The law said that everybody had to attend their local parish church.

The Church was organised in **ranks**. At the top was the King, also Supreme Head of the Church of England. Next came the Archbishop of Canterbury, then the other archbishops. The country was divided up into areas called **dioceses**, each diocese being run by a bishop. The dioceses were themselves divided into parishes, and the parishes each had a vicar or rector.

The Church of England cost a lot of money to run. To pay for itself it not only had the profits from its own land but also the **tithe**. This was like a modern tax. People had to give one tenth of their income to the Church. Some people, who could see how wealthy the Church was, were not happy about paying the tithe.

Until 1640 the Church had its own courts and its own prisons. The Church courts were responsible for a lot of what we would now call **morality**. Someone quarrelling with his or her wife or husband, committing adultery, spreading unpleasant gossip or even working on a saint's day (an official holiday) could find themselves charged in a Church court.

The Church and its courts also ran a system of censorship. Any book or pamphlet printed and sold had to be approved by the Church. Even teachers had to get a licence from their local bishop, so that the Church could be sure it approved of what would be taught to the young.

During James I's reign the Church of England had a new English translation of the Bible made. Usually called the **Authorised Version** (because its printing and sale were authorised by the King), this translation has remained in use until the present day.

What did people believe?

Not all Christians in Britain believed exactly the same thing. The group with the most separate beliefs were the Roman Catholics. The Church of England was a **Protestant** (non Roman-Catholic) Church. Most **Protestants** shared many key beliefs.

Predestination was their most important belief. This meant they believed that God knew what was going to happen. They believed people made their own decisions, but that God knew what they would decide. After all, if

---

Collected by Keith Thomas, in 'Religion and the Decline of Magic', 1971.

Source B

'Antichrist is permitted to rage against the elect. Yet his power stretches no further than to hurt their bodies. For a time God will permit this Antichrist to deceive the world. Read carefully, judge soberly, and pray to God for an understanding of this.'

From a note in the 'Geneva Bible', a translation used by many Puritans.

God was all-seeing and all-knowing, how could someone surprise Him? It followed that God knew whether someone would eventually go to heaven or not. Many people believed that if they prayed hard enough and long enough, God would tell them whether they would go to heaven. Most people who did this believed that God had told them they would go to heaven. They called themselves the **elect** or **saints**. We know of one or two people who went through this long period of prayer and became convinced they were not one of the elect.

Most Christians also believed that the world would end, perhaps in the near future. The Bible calls this the **Apocalypse**. It suggests that for many years **Antichrist** would triumph over the faithful. Soon after this, Christ would return and begin the **Millennium**, the thousand year rule of the saints. After this would come the final **Day of Judgement**. People spent much time trying to work out who Antichrist might be. Mathematicians tried to calculate when the end of the world would be, from clues given in the Bible.

The Puritans

Some people felt that the Church of England had got some things wrong. They felt it was not close enough to the church described in the Bible. Many of these people tried to change the Church from inside. They were often very strict in their religious and private lives. Some, however, thought the Church was too bad to change. They tried to set up their own private churches. They were often called **separatists** because they had separated themselves from the Church of England. They could be punished for not attending their parish church and they often objected to paying tithes. Some, like the **Pilgrim Fathers**, went to America to start colonies where they could worship as they liked. Despite the name, the Pilgrim Fathers were whole families. The colony wouldn't have had a future without women and children.

The Roman Catholics

Although **Catholicism** had been against the law in England since Elizabeth became Queen, there were still some Catholics. At times they were regarded as a possible danger, because they were meant to obey the Pope. The Pope wanted England to become Catholic again. He might support an invasion or rebellion that would make this happen. At times Catholics were often fined for not attending the Church of England, and some were even imprisoned. At other times, if they seemed loyal to the crown, they were allowed to live in relative peace.

Questions

Section A

1 Match the following words with their definitions:
   tithe   apocalypse   puritan

   a The name given by the Bible to the events leading up to the end of the world.
   b A person who believed that the Church of England was not strict enough.
   c Money paid to the Church of England to help pay for its costs.

2 Copy the following time-line, which shows the sequence of events for the Apocalypse, and fill in the labels from the phrases provided.

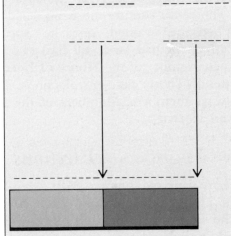

The Second Coming of Christ
The triumph of Antichrist
The thousand-year rule of the saints
The Day of Judgement

Section B

3 How do you think King James would have reacted to the suggestion that the Pope was Antichrist?

4 Sir Issac Newton (born 1642, died 1727) was probably the most famous scientist of the seventeenth century. He made many important scientific discoveries, including the law of gravity. How do you think he would have felt about scientists spending their time trying to work out the date of the Apocalypse from the clues in the Bible?

5 How do you think people would have felt about a neighbour who made up nicknames for them?

Parliament

Like many things in Britain, **Parliament** was not invented at one time. It gradually changed from the first meeting, on 27 January 1242, to the Parliament we have today. This change has not stopped. Recently some of Parliament's powers have been given to the European Community. Some of the most important changes took place in the seventeenth century. In other countries parliaments lost their power. In England, however, Parliament got much more powerful.

Calling a Parliament

When Parliament meets, it is said to be **sitting**. Now it sits all the time, except for holidays and elections. In the seventeenth century the King decided when to have one. When he wanted one he **summoned** Parliament. Parliament had (and still has) two parts, called **Houses**. Each member of the **House of Lords** got an invitation to attend. There were no elections; Lords were (and are) always members. Members of the **House of Commons** were elected.

Elections

There were two types of **MPs** (Members of Parliament) in the House of Commons. Each **county** chose two MPs. The election was held on one day and in one place. The only people who could vote were men who owned land worth more than £2. The sheriff would read out the names of the candidates, and people shouted for the MPs they wanted. The sheriff decided which men got the loudest shout, and they were elected. If he wasn't sure, he got the supporters of each man to stand together in groups. He then decided which was the biggest group. To actually count how many people wanted to vote for each man was very unusual.

The rest of the MPs were chosen by the **boroughs**. These were towns granted the right to send two MPs to parliament by the King. Boroughs had several different ways of choosing MPs. In most, just the town council could vote. In others, men who lived in certain houses could vote (usually the houses of the rich). In one or two boroughs, all adult men could vote.

What Parliament did

The King needed Parliament to agree to all **taxes**. New **laws** could be made only if Parliament agreed to them.

Source A

Dates when Parliament sat, 1603– 42

19 March to 7 July 1604
5 November 1605 to 27 May 1606
18 November 1606 to 4 July 1607
9 February to 23 July 1610
16 October to 6 December 1610
5 April to 7 June 1614
30 January to 4 June 1621
20 November to 18 December 1621
12 February to 29 May 1624
18 June to 11 July 1625
1 August to 12 August 1625
6 February to 16 June 1626
17 March to 26 June 1628
20 January to 10 March 1629
13 April to 5 May 1640
3 November 1640 to 20 April 1653

Questions

Section A

1 Draw a time-line from 1603 to 1640. Mark on it the times when Parliament was sitting.

Section B

2 For each of the following, say

   (i) what has changed between the seventeenth century and today and

   (ii) what difference you think this might make.

   a Calling Parliament.

   b Elections.

   c What Parliament does.

Kings and their ministers usually worked hard to get Parliament to do the things they wanted. This was all called **public business**. Parliament also dealt with **private business**. Permission to turn common land into fields, to make rivers passable to boats and even to get a divorce could be given only by Parliament. Most Parliaments spent about half of their time on private business. Without this it was very hard to get things done.

Parliament also looked into complaints about the way the country was governed. Sometimes it asked the King to change things. This was called the **consideration of grievances**. The House of Commons chose their own **Speaker**. He was the man who acted as a chairman – deciding who could speak and keeping order when the discussions got too noisy or out of hand.

The earliest picture of the House of Commons, 1624. The man on the large chair is the Speaker. The clerks, who kept a record of what was done, are at the table.

Source B

Family Life

Family life was dangerous during the seventeenth century. Almost one out of every three children died. Having children was also dangerous. Many women died during the birth or soon after.

Husbands and wives did not always marry for the reasons we choose to today. In rich families parents often chose their child's partner. This was partly because marriage was tied up with family money. Daughters were given a **dowry** by their parents. This was money or land which went to the new husband. Very rich families would make marriages with girls who could bring useful land or money as their dowry. In poorer families a dowry was less important, but parents still often made the choice. It was usual to give the possible husband and wife a chance to meet, and to refuse at least one suggested partner. The idea of marrying for love was seen as foolish. You can fall into and out of love quite quickly. The idea was that a couple should grow fond of one another after marriage.

Divorce was almost unknown. A divorce needed an Act of Parliament. Only seventeen divorces were passed between 1670 and 1750. The very poor, however, could sometimes change their partners. It was against the law, but the law was not always enforced. In some parts of the country this was done by **'wife sale'**. The husband would publicly offer his wife for sale. When she was bought, people accepted that she lived with the new 'husband'. This was not as cruel as it sounds. The three people concerned usually agreed before the sale, and nobody else would bid.

This does not mean that all marriages lasted for a long time. Death, not divorce, usually ended marriages early. In about the same number of families as today, either the father or the mother had been married before and there were step-children.

Family life, then, often meant arranged marriages and the death of many children. Some historians have looked at this and suggested there cannot have been much love in family life. One piece of evidence they use is the habit of giving a new baby the name of a brother or sister recently dead. Some families had three children with the same name. Usually only one was alive at a time. Other historians, paying more attention to diaries and family letters, think family life was just as likely to be affectionate then as now.

Source A

'In the average family of the seventeenth century, a man would be one of four, five or six children, two or three of whom would have died before the age of 15. At 26 or 27 he would marry a girl of 23 or 24 and have five or six children. Two or three would die young and the rest would be sent away from home at about the age of 12. After less than seventeen years there was a 50 per cent chance the marriage would end by the death of either himself or his wife.'

Lawrence Stone, 'The Family, Sex and Marriage in England, 1500–1800', 1979.

Source B

'My wife has much disappointed my hopes by bringing forth a daughter. She, finding herself not so welcome in this world as a son, has made a wise choice and gone to a better one.'

William Blundell, a gentleman, writing in 1653 about the birth and death of his sixth daughter and ninth child.

Source C

From a book of advice to women about how they should act as wives

'If you intend to be a good wife, and live comfortably, accept this. My husband is my superior and my better. He has authority and rules over me. Nature has given it to him. God has given it to him.'

W. Whately, 'The Bride Bush', 1617.

Source D

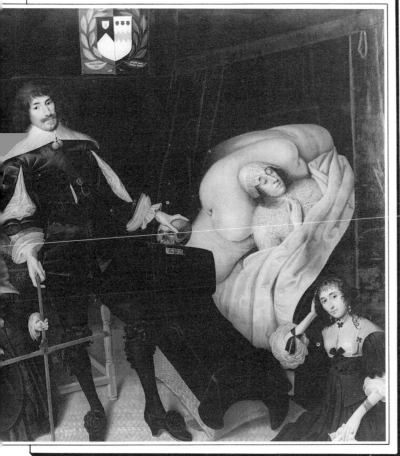

Sir Thomas Aston at the death bed of his wife, 1635.
She is also shown sitting at the foot of the bed. The
inscription on the cradle reads: he who hoped to reap
meat reaped bones.

Source E

'25 November. About eleven or twelve of the clock
my wife was with very sharp pains delivered of a
daughter, Jane. She was then 25 years of age
herself. Wife and child both well, praise be to my
good and merciful God.

30 November. God good to us in my wife and
babe's health, enabling her to nurse.

4 December. My dearest very ill, as if she would
have even died, but God continue us together to
praise him.

7 December. This week the Lord was good to me
and my family, in their health and preservation.

From the dairy of Ralph Josselin, an Essex vicar, 1645.

Source F

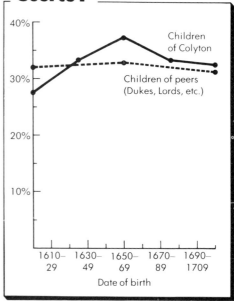

The percentage of children who died by
the age of 15. Colyton is a small village
in Devon.

Questions

Section A

1 What differences does Source F show
between the aristocracy and the
common people?

2 Why do some historians think there
was not much love in family life in
the seventeenth century?

3 What do Sources B and C suggest
about the life of women in the
seventeenth century?

Section B

4 Do you think Ralph Josselin would
have reacted in the same way as
William Blundell if his daughter had
died?

5 Does Source D suggest Sir Thomas
Aston cared about his wife and her
death?

6 Explain why you agree or disagree
with this statement:
'In the seventeenth century, family
life was different. There was very
little love.'

Medicine

The seventeenth century was an important time in the growth of **science**. Most important of all, it was the time when our modern way of looking at problems 'scientifically' was accepted.

There were important developments in **medicine**. In 1628 **William Harvey** showed that the heart pumped blood round the body. He also showed that the same blood kept circulating round and round. Before this most doctors thought that blood was a fuel like petrol and that it was somehow used and replaced with new blood. Harvey didn't just write a book telling people what he thought. He described experiments that others could also do, that proved his theory was right.

Many of the treatments used by doctors were based on ideas developed in Ancient Greece about 2,000 years before. The Greeks thought that healthy bodies had four liquids, which they called **humours**, each in balance with the others. If someone was ill, it was because their humours were not balanced. They might have too much or too little of one. The four humours were blood, phlegm, yellow bile and black bile. The way to make somebody better was to reduce the amount of one of the humours. This is why blood-letting was a treatment most doctors used. They thought that having too much blood might be the cause of the illness. Their treatment would be to cut a small vein and take out a cup of blood before allowing the cut to close.

Many doctors believed that the stars affected people's illnesses. They used zodiac charts, just like modern astrologers. Books told them which illnesses were influenced by which stars. Their treatments depended on the star concerned. Very often these people also believed in the four humours.

Not everyone went to a doctor if they were ill. Many people could not afford to, or they lived in small villages where there were no doctors. Women, sometimes called **wise-women**, also offered help and treatment. Their treatment was usually based on a mixture of common sense and tradition. As nobody knew what really caused illness, their treatments were probably no worse than a doctor's.

Childbirth was the one place where women were part of 'official' medicine. **Midwives**, who helped at a birth, were usually women. Practical experience was thought more important than any theoretical knowledge.

Source A

'*2 February*. His Majesty felt some unusual disturbance of the brain, soon followed by loss of speech and convulsions.

Two of the King's doctors opened a vein in his right arm, and drew off about 16 ounces of blood.

The rest of the doctors had a conference and prescribed three cupping glasses to be applied to his shoulders. About 8 ounces of blood were withdrawn.

So as to free his stomach of all impurities, they gave an emetic [to make him sick].

To leave no stone unturned, his hair was shaved and blistering agents were applied all over his head.

3 February. The doctors ordered sacred tincture every six hours. Meeting at noon they considered it necessary to open both jugular veins and draw off about 10 ounces of blood. At this point the King complained of a pain in the throat and a gargle was prescribed.

Further it seemed most desirable that his bowels should be kept continuously relaxed, by giving two ounces of sacred tincture.

4 February. It seemed advisable to the doctors to prescribe a mild laxative. As His Majesty's condition got worse during the night the doctors prescribed the following:

40 drops of spirit of human skull in an ounce and a half of Cordial Julep . . .

6 February. Alas, after an ill-fated night His Majesty's strength seemed exhausted. In spite of every kind of treatment attempted by doctors of the greatest skill, was seized quite unexpectedly by a mortal distress in breathing.'

From Sir Charles Scarburgh's account of the death of Charles II, 1685. He was one of the King's doctors.

Source B

The birth of a baby, late sixteenth century

Source C

'First, consider what planet causes the illness.

Second, consider what part of the body is affected by the illness.

Third, consider by what planet the affected part of the body is governed.

Fourth, you may treat the illness by herbs of the planet opposite to the planet that causes it.

Fifth, there is another way to cure illness. Every planet cures its own illness. The Sun and Moon, by their herbs, cure the eyes, Jupiter the liver.'

Nicholas Culpeper, 'The Complete Herbal', 1633.

Questions

Section A

1 Copy out the following sentences, rearranging the 'tails' so that each goes with the right 'head'

Heads	Tails
a In the seventeenth century science	the planets of the zodiac caused disease.
b William Harvey showed that	was becoming more important.
c Harvey described experiments so that	blood, phlegm, yellow bile and black bile.
d The four humours were	the same blood circulated round the body.
e Doctors thought people were ill	many poorer people when they were ill.
f Some doctors thought	if they had too much of one humour.
g Wise women treated	people could prove this for themselves.

Section B

2 How do you think seventeenth century people would have felt if they were offered modern drugs rather than blood-letting when they were ill? Give reasons for your answer.

3 The two doctors in Source B are studying the stars. How do you think seventeenth-century women would have felt about this behaviour? Give reasons for your answer.

4 Do you think the doctors in Source A were trying to kill Charles II? Give reasons for your answer.

The Reign of James I

A cartoon sold during James's reign. James is the man on the left. A plain countryman is asking James to chase away the courtiers who are weighing down his ass. James refuses.

When James became King of England, one group of his subjects was particularly happy. They were the **Puritans** – the people who thought the Church of England had not changed enough from the Roman Catholic Church, and who thought it should be much more strict. They were pleased because the Church in Scotland was much stricter than the English Church. They hoped James would set up the same type of Church in England.

One thousand churchmen signed a petition asking James to reform the Church of England. Their hopes were soon dashed. James called a conference at his palace at Hampton Court in 1604. As well as the Puritans, the people who were happy with the Church of England were there. The biggest disagreement was about the bishops. The Puritans wanted a church without bishops. They wanted the church to be run by committees. The bishops and their supporters thought the church needed to be run from the top. James agreed with the bishops and very little changed. The most important decision taken was to make a new translation of the Bible.

James also called a Parliament in 1604. He wanted to unite his two kingdoms of England and Scotland into one country with one Parliament. The English Parliament refused. England and Scotland continued to be two countries with separate Parliaments and laws, which just happened to share the same King.

There was also some trouble about the elections to Parliament. (See page 8 for a description of how elections were held.) Some defeated candidates claimed there had been cheating at their elections and asked that the true winners should be declared. James and the House of Commons argued about who should decide these cases. The House of Commons won. Since 1604 it has been accepted that only the House of Commons decides who has been elected as one of its members.

The difficult start to James's reign carried on. Many Catholics were worried about their position. They feared that, under James, they might be persecuted. A small group, which included **Guy Fawkes**, tried to blow up Parliament on 5 November 1605. They picked the only day when the King, the House of Lords and the House of Commons would be in the same room.

Historians usually divide James's problems up to make them easier to think about. He had problems to do with **religion**, problems because he did not have enough **money** to run the country, problems with **other countries**, and problems with his own **Parliaments**.

Questions

Section A

1   a How did James and his first Parliament disagree about elections?
    b What advantage would James have had if he had won that argument?
    c Do you think winning the argument would have helped James with some of the later problems in his reign? Give reasons for your answer.

	Religion	Money	Foreign affairs	Parliament
1603–1610				
1611–1619				
1620–1630				

Religion

The Puritans were still not happy with the Church of England. Most continued to go to the church services, but they often complained about what went on. Some set up their own churches. They had to do this secretly because it was against the law. A few left the country. In 1620 the Pilgrim Fathers went to the wilds of America to worship in the way they wanted to. (See pages 18–9).

Finance

Money was a big problem. James was expected to run the country on the customs duties and the profits from the royal lands. He was expected to need taxes only when there was a war. In fact it cost more than this to run the country, even in a quiet year. Parliament was not convinced, though. They thought the problem was caused by James giving away too much money to his favourites. In 1610 Parliament rejected a reform of the King's finances. He also failed to get the taxes he wanted from Parliament in 1614 and 1622.

Foreign affairs

James's problems with foreign affairs were tied up with religion and money. Europe was divided into Protestant and Catholic countries. The Catholic countries were more powerful. There seemed to be a danger that Protestantism would be destroyed by the Catholic countries. Many people in England felt that James should help the Protestants. They felt this especially after 1618. In that year a Protestant prince, married to James's daughter Elizabeth, had been driven out of Bohemia, where he had just been made King. Not only was Princess Elizabeth involved, but also this developed into the **Thirty Years' War**, a general war between Protestants and Catholics in Europe.

Parliament

All these problems got worse in Parliament. There were men in the two Houses who were Puritans, men who thought James wasted money and men who thought England should fight on the side of the Protestants in the Thirty Years' War. Parliaments complained about what was going on. They accused the King's favourites of dishonesty. They refused to grant him any taxes. Things got worse. There was a plan to marry Prince Charles, who would be the next King, to a Spanish princess. Spain was the leading Catholic power and had been England's enemy during Elizabeth's reign. None of these problems had really been solved when James died in 1625.

Section B

2 Draw up a grid like the one on the left. Mark on it, for each column, as many of the things mentioned in the text that come under that heading as you can. Some things may need to go in more than one column.

3 One of the things historians do is tell stories about the past. They try to explain what happened and why it happened. This is a bit like writing a story, because historians have to decide what order to tell things in. In this unit you have read about some of the problems James I had. At the start you read about early problems. Later you read about the problems divided into different themes (subject areas). History can be written either way. The important thing is to help readers understand.

a Using your grid as a guide, write the story of James's reign after 1610. Write about things in the order they happened. Do not group all the religious things together, and then all the financial things, in the way the text does.

b Which method do you think works best – writing by theme (like the text) or writing chronologically (as you did)? Give reasons for your answer.

15

The Gunpowder Plot

In 1605 James I was persuaded by his ministers to clamp down on the Catholics. Parliament was due to meet on 5 November. On 26 October **Lord Mounteagle**, a Catholic, was given a letter warning him not to go to the Parliament. Mounteagle gave the letter to James and his ministers, who ordered a search to be made of the cellars under Parliament. The searchers discovered a cellar full of gunpowder which could have been used to blow up the House of Lords. This was where the King, the Lords and most of the members of the House of Commons would be for the opening of Parliament. Also found in the cellar was a man who said his name was Johnson. Later it turned out that his name was **Guy Fawkes**.

Source A

'The King's kindness has ended in this. Catholic priests go openly about the country, saying Mass, and this gives great offence to others. Nothing can be done. The laws must be obeyed. We cannot hope for good government while we have a large number of people who obey foreign rulers, as Catholics do. The priests preach that the Catholics must do everything to help their religion even if it means killing the King.'

Source B

'It has pleased Almighty God to discover the most cruel and detestable plot. The plot was to kill the King, Queen, Prince, Council, Clergy, Judges and the principal gentlemen by secretly putting a great quantity of gunpowder into a cellar under Parliament, and so to have blown all up at a clap. God, out of his mercy and just revenge, allowed it to be discovered. The main plotter is one Johnson, a Yorkshire man and servant to Thomas Percy. This Percy had, about a year and a half ago, hired a house by Parliament, from which he had access to the cellar to store his wood and coal. He is a Catholic, and so is his man Johnson. Into this cellar Johnson had carried a great quantity of powder, all of which he had cunningly covered with firewood. On Tuesday at midnight, as he was busy to prepare his things for explosion, he was caught in the place itself. There was found some fine powder, to make a fuse. He would have saved himself from the blow by some half an hour.'

Source C

'He said he did not intend to set fire to the fuse until the King came into the House, and then he intended to do it so the gunpowder might more surely blow up a quarter of an hour later.'

From Guy Fawkes's confession, made after torture on 16 November 1605.

An ambassador from a Catholic country, writing home, reporting what had been said by Robert Cecil. Cecil was James I's chief minister, responsible for security.

Robert Cecil writing to the English Ambassador in Brussels, 9 November 1605.

Source D

A contemporary print of the execution of the plotters.

Questions

1 Why did Robert Cecil dislike the Catholics? Give reasons for your answer.

2 **a** Why did Cecil think that Percy was involved in the plot?
  b Why did Cecil think that Johnson was involved in the plot?

3 Does Guy Fawkes's confession (Source C) **confirm** Cecil's story (Source B)? Explain your answer.

4 'Most people in England were glad that the Gunpowder Plot failed, and came to hate the Catholics more because of it.' Does Source D support this view? Give reasons for your answer.

5 Is there enough evidence here to say who was responsible for the Gunpowder Plot? Explain your answer.

The Pilgrim Fathers

The story of the **Pilgrim Fathers** is quite well known. Persecuted for their religion, a group of Puritans left England on 5 August 1620. They had to turn back for repairs and left again on 6 September. They reached **Cape Cod**, in what is now the United States, on 9 November. On Christmas Day they started building their first houses. After a difficult first year, during which they worked very hard, they had a good harvest. They celebrated with a **Thanksgiving** dinner, and invited the local Indian tribes. This day is still celebrated as a public holiday in the USA.

Source A

A seventeenth-century print showing Puritans leaving England.

The first settlers

First of all, the name Pilgrim *Fathers* is wrong. The settlers were men, women and children. Secondly, many of the settlers had left England in 1608. They had been living in **Holland** where there was a treaty between the Catholics and the Protestants. This treaty meant that the English Puritans would be able to worship God in their own way. The treaty was due to end in 1621, and the English Puritans thought they might be persecuted. Some of these people decided to go to America. They sailed from Plymouth on the *Mayflower*. There were other people on the *Mayflower* who wanted to go and settle in America for other reasons. Some thought they would get rich. Others just wanted their own land to farm.

Where were they going?

The original plan was to go to somewhere near **Virginia**, in the south of the modern USA. The weather is good there. Cape Cod is in the north of the USA. The winters there are very cold indeed. About half of the settlers died during the first January and February, the coldest part of the winter.

Source B

'They were encountered many times with cross-winds and met with fierce storms. The ship was badly shaken and her upper parts made very leaky. One of the main beams in the midships cracked, which put them in some fear the ship would not be able to perform the voyage. In many of these storms the winds were so fierce and the storms so high, that the ship could not use any sail, but was forced to drift.'

William Bradford, 'History of the Plymouth Plantation, 1620−1651'. Bradford was one of the original settlers on the 'Mayflower'.

Source C

'After a long beating at sea they fell in with that land which is called Cape Cod. At which they were not a little joyful. After some discussion among themselves and with the master of the ship, they tacked southward. But after they had sailed that course for half a day, they fell amongst dangerous shoals and roaring breakers. They concieved themselves in great danger. They decided to go back to the Cape, and were happy to get out of danger before night.'

William Bradford, 'History of the Plymouth Plantation'.

Questions

Section A

1 Study Source A.

  a How does the source suggest that the people are leaving rather than just going for a walk?

  b Does the source suggest any reason why they are going?

  c How does the source suggest that the people are going to leave the country?

2 Does Source A prove that the Pilgrim Fathers went to America because they were afraid of what might happen to them in England?

Section B

3 Diagram 1 shows the first version of the story you read. Copy the diagram into your book.

4 Historians often talk about **causes** and **consequences**. For example, your history teacher might say: *'Jean didn't do her homework'*, so **Jean is in detention'**. The *italic text* is the cause, and the **bold text** is the consequence. On your copy of Diagram 1 shade in the causes in one colour, and the consequences in another. Make sure you add a key to say which is which.

5 Copy Diagram 2 into your book. **You will need to make the boxes bigger in your copy**. This time many of the boxes have not had their labels filled in. Fill in the missing labels from the choices below.

Ship not very safe.
Want to be rich or have own land to farm.
Rough sea crossing.
Not happy with Church of England.
Treaty ends. May not be safe in Holland.
Sea south of Cape Cod seems dangerous.

6 Give your copy of Diagram 2 a key, and shade the causes and consequences different colours.

Diagram 1

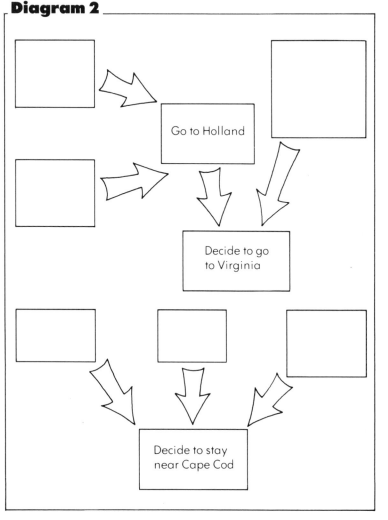

Diagram 2

Charles I

The democracy game

This unit starts with two games. The games will help you to understand the arguments during Charles I's reign. In both games there is a King and four other players. Most of the rules are the same for both games. The changes between Game 1 and Game 2 are the things to watch out for.

The games are about tax – how much tax players should pay the King. The King also has to give money back to the other players. Be careful with the time limit rule. If you don't agree before the time limit is up, everyone in your game loses. Your teacher will set the time limit.

Game 1

Aim: To agree how much tax should be paid to the King. There will be four rounds in which tax must be paid.

Rules:
1 There are five players – the King and players 1, 2, 3 and 4.
2 Players must keep their own score (how much money they have). It should be written down so that all players can see it. The King starts with £6. Players 1–4 start with £10 each.
3 Players 1, 2, 3 and 4 must all pay tax each round. They must all pay the same amount.
4 The King and **at least** three other players must agree on how much the tax should be for each round.
5 All money given in tax must be given back to players 1–4. The tax is divided by 5. If the number does not divide by 5, the King must add some so that it does. After the tax has been divided into five equal shares, Player 1 gets two shares; Players 2, 3 and 4 get one share each.

   For example, if the tax is £2, then the total tax will be £8. The King must add £2 so that it can be divided by 5. Player 1 will get £4; Players 2, 3 and 4 will get £2.

6 A copy of the tax form must be filled in for each round.
7 At the end of the game, any player who gets their target will be a winner. The targets are:

   King – keep score above £0.
   Player 1 – score £20 or more.
   Players 2, 3 and 4 – keep score above £7.

Game 2

Game 2 shares all the rules with Game 1 except:

4 The King and one other player must agree on how much tax there should be for each round.
5 All money raised in tax must be given back. The King can decide how to share it out. It does not have to be shared out equally.
7 The only change is for the King:
   The King – keep score above £0 and get Player 1's score above £20.

Game 1 Tax Form

Tax agreed	_____
Total tax collected	_____
King's contribution	_____
Money to be shared out	_____
(*Must end in 5 or 0*)	
One share =	_____
Player 1 gets	_____
Player 2 gets	_____
Player 3 gets	_____
Player 4 gets	_____

Game 2 Tax Form

Tax agreed	_____
Total tax collected	_____
King's contribution	_____
Money to be shared out	_____
(*Must end in 5 or 0*)	
Player 1 gets	_____
Player 2 gets	_____
Player 3 gets	_____
Player 4 gets	_____

Activities

1 a Who were the winners in Game 1?
  b Who were the winners in Game 2?

2 Rule 5 in Game 1 was meant to be like Parliament in Charles I's reign. How was it like Parliament?

3 Who was Player 1 supposed to be?

4 Divide Charles I's reign between 1625 and 1640 into two sections. Which years would be like Game 1?

Source A

Charles I soon fell out with his Parliaments. He quarrelled with the first one (1625) over taxes and his relations with Spain. Parliament granted Charles the customs duties for only one year. These taxes were usually granted to a new King for life. Charles quarrelled with his second Parliament (1626–7) over his favourite, the **Duke of Buckingham**. Many MPs thought that Buckingham had too much power over the King. They were also worried that much of the King's money was given to Buckingham and other favourites, rather than being used for the good of the country. The worst quarrel of all was with the Parliament of 1628–9. Buckingham was dead, but Parliament was still not happy with the King's government. Parliament criticised Charles for having Catholics at his court, for raising taxes without its permission, for changes in the Church of England and for his foreign policy. Finally the Parliament complained about Charles trying to interfere with it. Charles dismissed this Parliament and tried to govern without one.

The next eleven years, when there was no Parliament, are sometimes called the **Eleven Years' Tyranny**. Charles had to find ways of getting money. He did this by bending the law. One tax he used was called Ship Money. This was supposed to be for the navy, and only towns near the coast had paid. Charles made all the country pay. Many people objected. They thought it was not right for Charles to raise money without Parliament agreeing.

One of Charles's chief ministers was **William Laud**, Archbishop of Canterbury. Laud was changing the Church of England as well as helping Charles rule without Parliament. He was making it more like the Roman Catholic Church, even less like the Church the Puritans wanted.

A contemporary cartoon of Laud, Bastwick, Burton and Prynne. Bastwick, Burton and Prynne criticised Laud's changes in the Church. They were arrested in 1637. They were tried in the Star Chamber, a special court where Charles's ministers, including Laud, were the judges. There was no jury. The three were found guilty and sentenced to have their ears cut off and their cheeks branded.

Questions

1 a Which man in the cartoon is Laud?
  b What do you think the two men standing behind the table with muskets are supposed to be?
  c What is being eaten?
  d Do you think the artist supported Laud?

2 Why might many people think the trial of Bastwick, Burton and Prynne was not fair?

3 How could people complain about things they thought were unfair? (Look back to page 9.)

4 a Why did many people think they needed a Parliament?
  b Why might some people have been happy without one?

Scotland and Ireland

The Arch-Prelate of St Andrewes in Scotland reading the new Service-booke in his pontificalibus assaulted by men & Women, with Cricketts stooles Stickes and Stones.

A contemporary print about events in Scotland.

'29 April 1639. Our Army is weak; our purse is weaker. If we fight with these forces early in the year we shall have our throats cut. If we delay fighting long we cannot, for want of money, keep our Army together. I dare say there was never so raw, so unskilful and so unwilling an army brought to fight. As yet they are as like to kill their fellows as the enemy.'

From a letter by Sir Edmund Verny, Charles I's standard bearer, who was with the army raised to fight the Scots.

Scotland

The Church in Scotland was a very strict Protestant one, called **Presbyterian**. Charles I wanted to make it less strict, like the Church of England. In July 1637 he ordered that all church services should be taken from a new prayer book, prepared by his English archbishop, William Laud. Most Scots wanted to keep their Presbyterian Church. There was a riot in St Giles' Cathedral, Edinburgh, when the new prayer book was first used.

After the riot a group called the **Covenanters** took over Scotland. A covenant is an agreement. The Covenanters agreed to stick together and defend the Presbyterian Church. In 1639 Charles attacked with an English army. The Scots won easily. Without a lot of money Charles could not raise a better army. He could not get more money without a Parliament. In 1640 he called his first Parliament for eleven years, to get money to fight the Scots Covenanters.

Driuinge Men Women & children by hund: reds vpon Briges & casting them into Riuers, who drowned not were killed with poles & shot with muskets.

G

Mr Blandry Minister hanged after pulled his flesh from his bones in his wiffes sight

H

A contemporary print about the Irish Rebellion.

Ireland

In Ireland most of the poorer people, and many of the rich, were Catholic. The country was divided between Catholics and Protestants, and also between English settlers and families who had been there for a long time. There had also been rebellions against English rule and against Protestantism.

Charles I sent one of his best ministers, the **Earl of Strafford**, to rule Ireland. Strafford ruled Ireland harshly, but he was a success. He got the Catholics and Protestants to co-operate. He made sure the Irish Parliament always agreed with his policies. He even raised a strong army in Ireland, which could have been used to fight the Scots. But this worried many people in England. Strafford wanted Charles to rule without a Parliament in England. His Irish army was mainly Catholic. Many English were scared that Charles might use Strafford's army against them.

The English Parliament, which met in 1640, arrested Strafford and tried him for treason. With Strafford gone, a rebellion broke out in Ireland. This time it was a Catholic rebellion and many Protestants were cruelly murdered. Charles needed to raise an army to put down this rebellion.

Diagram 1: Scotland ___ Diagram 2: Ireland

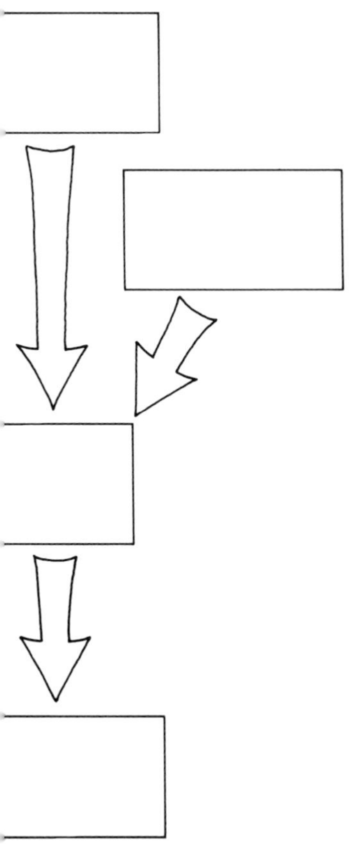

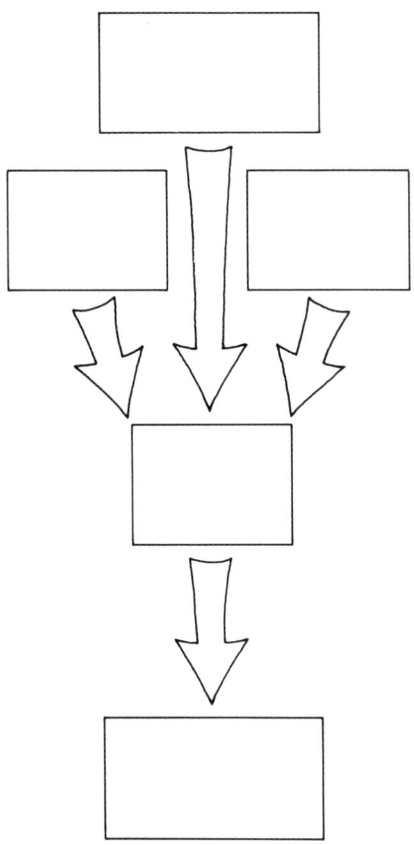

Section A

1 Does Source A prove that the riot was about the new prayer book?

2 a What does Source B tell you about Charles's army in 1639?
   b Do you think Sir Edmund Verny would be a be a reliable witness? Give reasons for your answer.

3 Are the people being ill-treated in Source C Protestants or Catholics?

4 What did the artist of Source C want people to think about the Irish rebellion? Give reasons for your answer.

Section B

5 Copy Diagram 1 into your book. Fill in the labels from the choices below.

   Rebellion.

   Charles wanted new church services.

   Most Scots wanted to keep their Presbyterian Church.

   Charles needed to raise an army.

6 Copy Diagram 2 into your book. Fill in the labels from the choices below.

   Rebellion.

   Many Irish disliked English rule.

   Many Irish were Catholics.

   Charles needed to raise an army.

   Irish ruled harshly by Strafford.

7 Make a key for Diagrams 1 and 2 and shade in the boxes that are **causes** and those that are **consequences**. Are there any boxes that are both? Explain why.

The Long Parliament

*Political cartoon of 1641. Charles I had used **monopolies** as a way of getting money. A monopoly was created when only one person or company was allowed to make or sell one particular thing. Parliament thought monopolies were wrong. This cartoon shows Alderman Abel, who had a wine monopoly.*

Having lost his war against the Scots in 1639, Charles was determined to fight again and win in 1640. He could not do this without a lot of money to pay for his army. The only thing to do was call a Parliament. The House of Commons would not vote taxes to help Charles fight the war unless he agreed to govern the country in a way they approved of. Charles quickly ended the Parliament (called ever since the **Short Parliament**) and hoped a war against Scotland would make people support him anyway.

The fighting in the summer of 1640 was a disaster. The Scots invaded northern England. Charles agreed to pay all the costs of the Scots' army as well as his own. Their army would not leave until they got their money. Charles had to call another Parliament.

This one is called the **Long Parliament**. It kept sitting until 1653, and some of its members came back again in 1659 and 1660. This time Charles had to listen to the complaints of the House of Commons. He had to get taxes from the Parliament to pay his debts (and make the Scots go home). A group of MPs and Lords led by **John Pym** were determined to use this chance to make sure Charles could never again try to govern without Parliament.

Many of Charles's ministers were scared and fled overseas. His most important ministers, the Earl of Strafford and Archbishop Laud, were arrested for treason. Laud was left a prisoner in the Tower of London. Strafford was put on trial for treason. The penalty was death.

Most MPs supported Pym. Most were glad Strafford was no longer a powerful minister. But this was not the same thing as proving he had committed treason. The trial went badly for Pym. None of the evidence was convincing. It looked as if Strafford would be found innocent. Pym changed his tactics. He proposed an **Act of Attainder** against Strafford. This is a special Act of Parliament which says the person named was guilty of treason. This means it had to pass in the House of Commons and the House of Lords, and be agreed by the King. All Pym had to do was get the Act passed. The Commons passed it with some argument. The Lords passed it only when there was a demonstration outside Parliament by an anti-Strafford mob. Some Lords who would have voted against the Act were too scared to go into Parliament. Charles said he would never agree to it. Mobs kept demonstrating against Strafford, and Strafford himself advised Charles to agree. Otherwise there might be a revolution. Charles agreed, and Strafford was executed on 12 May 1641.

Sir Edward Hyde talks to the Earl of Essex about Strafford.

Hyde later became a Royalist, while Essex was Parliament's first general. In April 1641 they talked about what should be done with Strafford. Hyde suggested he should be fined and permanently banned from government. Essex did not agree . . .

'He shook his head and answered: "Stone-dead hath no fellow. If he were fined and imprisoned during his life, the King would grant him his pardon, release all fines, and give him his liberty as soon as he wanted his service; which would be as soon as the Parliament was ended."'

Edward Hyde, Earl of Clarendon, 'A History of the Great Rebellion.' Hyde wrote this passage in the 1660's.

Source C

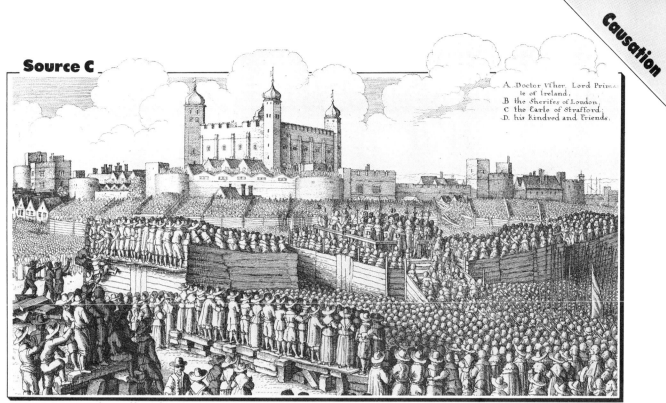

A. Doctor Vher, Lord Prima
te of Ireland,
B the Sherifes of London,
C the Earle of Strafford,
D. his kindred and Friends,

The execution of Strafford from a print sold at the time.

Questions

Section A

1 Write out this list of events in chronological order:
Execution of Strafford.
First meeting of the Long Parliament.
The Scots winning the war of 1640.
The Short Parliament.

2 **a** What was a monopoly?
b Did the artist of Source A think monopolies were a good thing?

3 **a** Why did Essex think Strafford should be killed?
b Does Source C suggest that most Londoners agreed with him?

Section B

4 Copy the cause-and-consequence diagram into your book. Fill in the boxes from the choices below.
The Scots defeated Charles.
Charles called Parliament.
Charles called another Parliament.
Charles needed money to pay the Scots.
Charles dismissed Parliament.

5 Things were not as simple as this diagram suggests. For instance, box 3 is a cause of box 5. Explain why this is.

6 Explain why the event in box 4 would not have happened without those in boxes 1 and 2.

7 There are other important causes not in the diagram. For instance:
Many people were not happy with the way Charles I ruled England.
Many did not approve of the changes in the Church that Laud and Charles wanted.

Draw a new diagram. Use the new causes and make more links between the others.

1 | Charles needed money for war against the Scots
⇩
2 |
⇩
3 | Parliament would not support the war
⇩
4 |
⇩
5 | Charles did not have enough money for his army
⇩
6 |
⇩
7 |
⇩
8 |

25

The Start of the Civil War

Source A

A political cartoon. Laud and another bishop are shown in the Tower of London. Finch and Windebanke were two of Charles's ministers between 1629 and 1640. The Deputy was Strafford. Two clergymen are in a booth at Lambeth Fair. Wine had been a monopoly before Parliament returned in 1640.

Between the execution of Strafford in May 1641 and going to Scotland in August Charles agreed to many **reforms**. The most important were a law that there must be a Parliament at least once every three years and a law that Charles could not end the Long Parliament until it agreed. He also accepted that most of his schemes to get money during the Eleven Years' Tyranny were illegal. Most of Charles's ministers from 1629 to 1640 were in prison or had fled abroad. They were often replaced by men trusted by parliament. Even John Pym was offered a job in the government.

It is important to realise that nobody wanted a civil war when the Long Parliament first met. Pym and his allies wanted Parliament to be much more important. Most MPs wanted to change the way England had been ruled between 1629 and 1640. Charles wanted to preserve as much of his power as he could, and also to prevent the Puritans from influencing the Church of England. Many Puritans wanted the Church of England to change, and they wanted to be allowed to set up their own churches and worship in their own way.

This leaves us with a problem. Nobody wanted a civil war. Most people had got most of what they wanted by the summer of 1641. Why then was there a civil war? There is a clue in Source B on page 24. The problem for Pym and his supporters was simple. Could they trust Charles?

Activities

1 **a** What was Source A celebrating?
  b Can you suggest when in 1641 Source A might have been sold? Give reasons for your answer.

2 In the seventeenth century people counted the new year from March, not January. January was one of the last months of the old year. Printers often used an 'f' for an 's'. What was Pym's speech about?

3 What were the names of the Five Members?

4 **a** Write out the text of Source C.
  b Do you think the author of Source B supported Parliament or the King? (**Cavaliers** was a name given to Charles's supporters.)

5 Why do you think these three sources were printed and published?

Source B

Maſter PYM
HIS SPEECH
In *Parliament*, on *Wedneſday*, the fifth of *January*, 1641,
Concerning the Vote of the Houſe of *Commons*, for his diſcharge upon the Accuſation of High Treaſon, exhibited againſt himſelfe, and the Lord *Kimbolton*, Mr. *Iohn Hampden*, Sr. *Arthur Hiſlerig*, Mr. *Stroud*, M. Hollis, by his Maieſty.

The true Effigies of Mr. Iohn Pym, Eſquire

London Printed for I.W. 1642.

Pamphlet, 1642.

Source C

A true and exact Relation of the manner of his Maieſties ſetting up of His Standard at *Nottingham*, on Munday the 22. of Auguſt 1642.

Firſt, The forme of the Standard, as it is here figured, and who were preſent at the advancing of it

Secondly, The danger of ſetting up of former Standards, and the damage which enſued thereon.

Thirdly, A relation of all the Standards that ever were ſet up by any King.

Fourthly, the names of thoſe Knights who are appointed to be the Kings Standard-bearers. With the forces that are appoynted to guard it.

Fifthly, The manner of the Kings comming firſt to *Coventry*.

Sixthly, The *Cavalieres* reſolution and dangerous threats which they have uttered, if the King concludes a peace without them, or hearkens unto his great Councell the Parliament: Moreover how they have ſhared and divided *London* amongſt themſelves already.

Nottingham.

Pamphlet, 1642.

Questions

Section A

1 a Draw a time-line of events from 1640 to 1642.
 b Mark the point when you think the Civil War became something that was likely to happen.
 c Give reasons for your choice.

Section B

2 What did the following people want when the Long Parliament first met?
 a John Pym.
 b Most MPs.
 c King Charles.

3 There was a civil war. Does this mean that what people wanted does not matter at all? Give reasons for your answer.

While they were worrying about this the **Irish Rebellion** started (see pages 22–3). People were shocked by the news of the killing in Ireland. The Irish rebels claimed that Charles supported their rebellion, although this was not true. Even people who did not think Charles was involved in the Irish Rebellion wondered if he could be trusted with an army to put it down. He might use it to get rid of the English Parliament first.

Charles returned from Scotland on 25 November. On 4 January 1642 he tried to arrest the **Five Members** – his leading opponents in Parliament. They had already left, but this was a great shock. How could Parliament discuss the country's problems if the King might force his way in with armed men and arrest people who criticised him?

Crowds in London demonstrated in defence of Parliament. Charles thought it would be safer to leave the city. In February the Queen went abroad to raise money for Charles. In April Sir John Hotham, a supporter of Parliament, would not let Charles into Hull, where all the arms from the war with Scotland were stored. In June both sides started to raise soldiers, and on 22 August Charles I raised his standard, the traditional declaration of war.

Fighting in the Civil War

When the quarrel between the King and Parliament turned into a fight, there were not many trained soldiers to do the fighting. There had not been serious fighting in England since 1487. Nor had there been any major wars against foreign countries in most people's lifetimes. The few men who knew about war had learned by fighting abroad. **Drill books** (books telling soldiers how to fight), were bestsellers during 1642. Both Sources C and E come from such books.

The books all described a perfect system. In England there were not enough of the right type of weapons to follow the advice. At the first battle, **Edgehill**, about four hundred of the Royalist musketeers only had wooden clubs – there weren't enough muskets.

Soldiers were divided into three types: **cavalry**, who fought on horseback, and **pikemen** and **musketeers**, who fought on foot.

Cavalry were supposed to have pistols or short muskets. They were to be trained to fight mainly by firing these and moving away quickly before the enemy could get them. At the start of the war most English cavalry just had swords. They fought hand to hand with them instead. Cavalry were thought to be the most powerful soldiers on the battlefield.

Pikemen and musketeers needed to be trained to work together. The musketeers could shoot the enemy. The pikemen kept the musketeers safe from the enemy cavalry.

Source A

'Cromwell's men were armed and mounted not unlike heavy cavalry of later days. They wore a triple-barred lobster-tailed helmet, or pot, back and breast plates, and a buff coat. Their weapons included a long, stiff straight sword and a pair of pistols. They did not have carbines. Cromwell's men were trained to advance to the attack, riding knee to knee, at "a good round trot". The idea was to keep the men firmly under control so as to enable them to rally quickly after fighting.'

Peter Young, 'Oliver Cromwell', 1968.

Source B

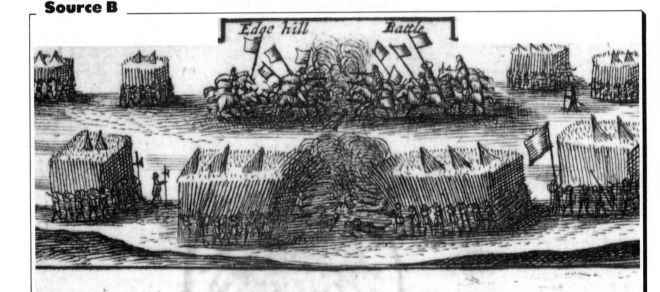

From a Royalist book describing the early events of the war, May 1643.

Source C

Some of the movements for a musketeer, from a drill book from the time of the Civil War.

Source D

'A pikeman was chosen for his height and stature, as it needed a strong person to wield the 18-foot-long pike. Pikemen formed the central body of the army, and by square formation protected the musketeers from a cavalry attack. In the case of heavy cavalry attacks the pike was held in the left hand, with the end against the inside of the right foot, and the point lowered in front. In the case of a light cavalry attack, the pikeman would hold the pike at shoulder level, parallel to the ground, and charge the attackers.'

R. Potter and G. A. Embleton, 'The English Civil War', 1973.

Source E

Some of the movements for a pikeman, from a drill book from the time of the Civil War.

Questions

1 What types of soldiers can you see in Source B? Describe what each is doing.

2 **a** What does the musketeer do with his 'match' in Source C? (The match is the cord lighted at both ends.)
   b Does Source C help explain why musketeers took a long time between each shot? Explain your answer.

3 Why were pikemen usually big men?

4 For each source, say whether it is a primary or a secondary source and give a reason for your choice.

5 Do you think the authors of Source D must have seen the drill book from which Source E is taken?

6 Which of these sources are most useful in helping you understand what fighting in the Civil War must have been like? Give reasons for your answer.

The Civil War 1642–44

The first great battle of the Civil War, **Edgehill** in 1642, was a draw. The fighting that year ended with Charles in **Oxford**. He tried to capture London, and got as far as Turnham Green (now a station on the London Underground). There, however, his army was so outnumbered by Parliament's forces that he retreated without fighting.

In 1643 Charles planned a triple attack on London with his armies from the North, the West and Oxford. The plan failed. All three armies got held up trying to capture towns in their own area. That winter Parliament made a treaty with the Scots. In return for an army, Parliament agreed to set up a Scots-style Presbyterian Church in England.

In 1644 Parliament had a chance to win the war. At **Marston Moor** the Scots and two of Parliament's armies, that of the North and the Eastern Association, beat **Prince Rupert** and destroyed his army. Until then Rupert had been the most successful Royalist general. In the South, Parliament sent two armies to defeat the King and capture Oxford. The generals would not work together, and Charles was able to beat each separately. Charles's success in the south evened out his loss in the North.

While all this was going on, the country was changing. The old order was breaking down. The Church was no longer able to control things. Lots of groups set up their own churches, often with ideas very few would approve of. Both sides published newspapers and pamphlets full of **propaganda** to convince people to support them.

Source A

Source B

Part. III.   *for the CAVALLRIE.*

CHAP. XI.

Of spies.

THe best and principall means for a Commander to avoid divers inconveniences, and to effect many worthy designes, are First ᵃ to be sure to keep his own deliberations and resolutions secret. ᵇ Secondly, to penetrate the designes and intentions of the enemie. For which purpose it behoveth him to have good spies, which must be exceeding well rewarded, that so they may be the readier to expose themselves to all dangers. The best and most assured spies are ones own souldiers, which (feigning some discontent for want of pay or otherwise) enter into the enemies service, and get themselves into the Cavallrie, as having best opportunitie (whether in the field or in garrison) to give information. Of these it is good to have many, and in severall places, the one knowing nothing of the other. You are to agree with them of the place where they shall convey their letters as some tree, gallows, or other place easie to finde, where they also shall finde yours, giving them order to come in person when their advice is of great importance: as, if the enemie would fall upon a quarter, surprise some place, or attempt some other great enterprise. There might also divers souldiers be daily sent disguised, under severall pretences, to observe what is done in the enemies leaguer, when it is neare. The boores use also to serve for spies, as we women as men, which, being not much regarded nor suspected, may have the freer accesse: but these are not alwaies to be trusted, neither are they so well able to judge of or to pierce into businesse, and the lesse assurance and information is to be had by their relations.

There are also spies which are called double, which must be men of great fidelitie. These (to get credit with the enemie) must sometimes give him true information of what passeth on the other side; but of such things and at such times, as they may do no hurt. But the king

M

'Militarie Instructions for the Cavallrie', 1632, reprinted 1644.

A print showing Royalist soldiers, published by supporters of Parliament during the war.

Source C

Description of the Royalist's capture of Birmingham

'Having thus possessed themselves of the Town, they ran into every house cursing and damning, threatening and terrifying the poor Women most terribly, setting naked Swords and Pistols to their breasts, they fell to plundering all the Town before them. Picking purses and pockets, searching in holes and corners. Tiles of houses, wells, pools, cellars, gardens, and every other place they could suspect for money or goods, forcing people to deliver all the money they had. They beastly assaulted many women's chastity, and impudently made their brags of it afterwards, how many they had ravished; glorying in their shame. That night few or none went to bed, but sat up revelling, robbing, and tyrannising over the poor frightened women and prisoners, drinking drunk healths to Prince Rupert's dog.

Nor did their rage here cease, but when the next day they were to march away from the Town, they used all possible diligence in every street to kindle fire with gunpowder, match, wisps of straw, hay, burning coals etc. flung into any places where it was likely to catch hold.'

'Prince Rupert's Burning Love to England, discovered in Birmingham's Flames', 1643.

Source D

Title page from 'The Bloody Prince', 1643.

Questions

Section A

1 Write a paragraph about the war in each year, 1642–1644.

2 According to Source B:
   a What two things should a commander do to be successful?
   b Who make the best spies?
   c What are the good and bad points of women spies?

Section B

3 Do you think historians studying the Civil War will find Source B useful? Give reasons for your answer.

4 a What are the soldiers doing in Source A?
   b Are there any reasons why this source might not be true?

5 a Does the author of Source E agree with women preaching?
   b Why do you think Source E was published?
   c Do you think Source E told the truth?

6 a Was Source C was written by a Royalist or a supporter of Parliament?
   b Do Sources C and D support each other?
   c Does Source A support Sources C and D?
   d Do Sources A, C and D **prove** that the Royalists were cruel and mistreated their enemies?

Source E

Title page of a pamphlet, 1641.

The New Model Army

Activities

1 How big were the armies at Naseby?

2 How big does Source A make each army look?

3 How far apart do the armies look in Source A?

4 Do you think this is likely to have been true? Give reasons for your answer.

5 Is Source A biased? Explain your answer.

6 a Give an example of something you think Source A might be reliable about.

  b Give an example of something you think Source A might not be reliable about.

Parliament was dismayed by its failure to win in 1644. During the winter there were bitter quarrels. The generals, who were mainly members of the House of Commons or House of Lords, blamed one another. It was agreed eventually to scrap the old armies and most of the old generals. The **New Model Army**, was set up. MPs and Lords were banned from holding commands in this army. The new general, **Sir Thomas Fairfax**, got special permission for one MP, **Oliver Cromwell**, to command the cavalry.

The Royalists were scornful of the New Model, and were keen to fight. Despite being outnumbered about 9,000 to 14,000, they attacked at **Naseby** on 14 June. The way the two armies lined up can be seen in Source A. Rupert, on the Royalist right, charged and broke Ireton's

Source A

A Description of His MAJESTIE'S ARMY of Horse and Foot, and of his Excellencies Sᵗ THOMAS FAIREFAX: as they were drawn into severall Bodies at the BATTAIL of NASBIE June the 14ᵗʰ 1645.

The Battle of Naseby, from a print published in 1647.

Source B

*A print published in 1646. The Ark has carried Parliament and
the Assembly of ministers through the Royalist flood.*

cavalry in front of him. Rupert's men carried on until they got to the Parliamentary baggage train. In the centre the two sets of infantry were stuck in fierce hand-to-hand fighting, with the Royalists slowly pushing the Parliamentarians back. On the other side Cromwell made the decisive breakthrough. His cavalry crushed the Royalists in front of them. Cromwell kept some cavalry back while the rest chased the beaten Royalist horse. He used this cavalry to charge the Royalist infantry in the rear. They were trapped. The battle was soon over, with the Royalist infantry destroyed. About 4,500 were prisoners, and the rest were dead.

Naseby saw the end of the King's last great army. The New Model Army quickly won the war. It beat the only other large Royalist force at the **Battle of Langport**, before capturing Bristol, the Royalists' second most important city. Oxford was not captured until 1646, but from Naseby onwards there could be little doubt who would win the war.

Questions

Section A

1 a List the names of the Royalists who are threatening the ship in Source B.
 b Who is missing?
 c Why do you think this is?

Section B

2 a Draw a plan of the armies at the start of the Battle of Naseby.
 b Tell the story of the battle, using more plans to show the different incidents.

3 Using the material on pages 26–31, tell the story of the Civil War from 1642 to 1646.

1647: Year of Revolution

The democracy game again

This is the same game you played in Unit 1.10. You will use the rules printed for Game 1 there, except for the changes given here.

Game 3

1 There are five players. the MPs, the Voter and players 1, 2 and 3.
2 The MPs and the Voter start with £20 each. Players 1, 2 and 3 start with £5 each.
4 The MPs and the Voter decide how much tax should be paid each round.
5 All money raised in tax must be given back. The MPs decide how to share it out. It does not have to be shared out equally.
6 At the end of the game any player who gets their target will be a winner. The targets are:

MPs and Voter: score £27 or more.
Players 1, 2 and 3: score more than £2.

Game 4

1 There are five players. Voters 1, 2, 3, 4, and 5.
2 Voter 1 starts with £20. Voter 2 starts with £15. Voter 3 starts with £10. Voters 4 and 5 start with £5.
3 All players pay tax each round. They must all pay the same amount.
4 Your teacher will set the tax for each round.
5 All the tax must be given back to the players each round. The players must agree how the money should be divided. It need not be divided equally. If the players cannot agree they can vote. Any division with three votes or more is the one chosen.
7 Targets: all players to have at least as much money as they started with.

Activities

The problem for the players in the games is like one of the big problems in 1647. How could people be sure Parliament would be fair?

In 1647 there had not been an election since 1640. Many MPs were dead or were banned from Parliament because they had been Royalists. Even if there were new elections, only the richer men would be able to vote. The **Levellers** spoke up for the poor. They said that Parliament would be fair only if it was elected by all men. Nobody seriously suggested women should have the vote.

1 What does this tell us about the position of women in 1647?

2 How does Game 3 represent a Parliament where only the rich could vote?

3 Which player or players have the best chance of winning in Game 3?

4 How does Game 4 represent a Parliament where all men got the vote?

5 Which player or players have the best chance of winning in Game 4?

6 Which of these systems seems the fairer?

Source A

The Agreement of the People

'We do now hold ourselves bound to each other, to take the best care we can for the future, to avoid the danger of returning to a slavish condition. . . We declare that the People should choose themselves a Parliament every two years; that the power of this Parliament is inferior only to the people's . . . Parliament should not have the power to be compulsive in matters of religion . . . . Impressing (conscripting) any to serve in the wars is against our freedom. . . That in all Laws made, every person may be bound alike. . . That as the Laws ought to be equal, so they must be good.'

Source B

'The poorest he that is in England has a life to live, as the greatest he.'

Colonel Rainborough speaking during one of the Army debates on 'The Agreement of the People'.

Written by the Levellers, 1647.

Source C

Ieſuit   *Adamite*   *Libertin*   *Anabaptist*   *Ante Scripturian*

Prints from a pamphlet about the different types of Independent churches that had grown up, 1647.

Revolution

In 1647 the Civil War became a **revolution**. Parliament's supporters started arguing among themselves. Some wanted the King restored with most of his old powers. Some wanted a Presbyterian Church like the Church in Scotland. Others wanted all people to be free to join any church they liked (they were called **Independents**). It had been easy to be against what was wrong. It was not so easy to agree on what was right.

The country had changed since 1640. There was much more freedom. Independents had set up churches everywhere. People were used to much more freedom. Many were shocked by the things that went on. They wanted a strong government to stop them. Others liked their new freedom and would fight to keep it.

Tax and the Army brought the crisis to a head. Parliament decided to get rid of most of the Army, it cost too much to keep. Most soldiers who were kept were going to be sent to Ireland. The Army refused to be disbanded. Many soldiers were owed six months' pay. They thought they had a better chance of getting the money if they stuck together. Others, many of them also Levellers, said they had fought to make England a free country, and they were going to make sure it became one. They demanded fresh elections and a **constitution**. They published their ideas in a statement called **The Agreement of the People**.

The Army stayed together. Officers and men representing all the regiments met and debated what the Army should do. In the end it marched on London and stopped some MPs from going to Parliament. This meant that Independents were in control of Parliament.

The Army and the Independents were still debating what to do when, in 1648, there was a Royalist rising. The **Second Civil War** had begun. Decisions could wait until the war was won.

Questions

Section A

1 What do you think Rainborough meant (Source B)?

2 a What is the Libertin (Libertine) doing in Source C?
   b Do you think the publisher of Source C supported the idea of more freedom?

Section B

3 Having won the war, the Army turned against Parliament.

   a Describe a religious cause for this.
   b Describe a financial cause for this.
   c Describe a political cause for this.

4 Do you think each of these causes was equally important, or might one have been more important than others? Give reasons for your answer.

Trial and Execution of Charles I

Charles I was not the first English king to be killed by his subjects. Edward II and Richard II had been quietly murdered. Charles, however, was put on trial for crimes against the people, found guilty and publicly executed. This was a very different sort of king killing.

In 1647, Charles was a prisoner of Parliament. However, Parliament itself was split into different groups. Charles tried to negotiate with all of them. At the same time, he secretly planned a new civil war. He arranged for the Scots to change sides. In 1648 their army invaded England to fight for Charles. At the same time there were Royalist uprisings in various parts of England.

The Second Civil War was soon over. The New Model Army was too strong for both the Scots and the Royalists. The generals, especially Cromwell, blamed Charles for all the death and injury because his plotting had caused this war. They were also convinced that Charles could not be trusted not to start another war. The only way to be safe was to get rid of Charles.

The Presbyterians in Parliament could not imagine England without a king or queen. After the war they made a deal with Charles called the **Treaty of Newport**. This would have given Charles many of his old powers back, almost as if the civil wars had not happened. This was too much for the Army. If Parliament could not be trusted to deal with Charles, the Army would have to start by dealing with Parliament.

Pride's Purge took place on 6 December 1648. Colonel Pride stood outside the House of Commons with some soldiers. He stopped most Presbyterian MPs from going in, and arrested their leaders. Those MPs who were left, called the **Rump**, soon agreed that Charles should be tried for his crimes. A special **High Court of Justice** was appointed, because no court had the power to try a king. Charles was accused of being 'a tyrant, traitor, and murderer, and a public and implacable enemy to the Commonwealth of England.' He would not accept the court had the power to try him. The court went ahead, however, found Charles guilty and sentenced him to death by beheading.

The execution was on 30 January 1649. There was a large crowd, but they had to wait until Parliament passed another Act saying it was illegal to proclaim a new king. Charles was very brave, asking the executioner to wait until he finished his prayer. His head was cut off with one blow. The troubled reign of Charles I was over.

Source A

Richard Bradshaw, the Judge at Charles I's trial, had this hat specially made. It was reinforced with metal.

Source B

On the day of his execution, which was Tuesday 30 January, I stood amongst the crowd in the street before Whitehall Gate, where the scaffold was erected, and saw what was done. The blow I saw given, and I remember well, there was such a groan by the thousands then present, as I never heard before and desire I may never hear again. [Troops were sent] purposely to master the people, and to disperse and scatter them, so that I had much ado amongst the rest to escape home without hurt.

From the Diary of Philip Henry, a young man with a Royalist background.

Activities

1   Does Source A prove the trial of Charles I was unpopular?

2   a   How does Source B suggest the Army thought there might be trouble at the execution?
    b   Does Source C support this?

3   Does Source C suggest the execution was popular or unpopular?

4   Can you say, **on the evidence of these sources**, whether the trial and execution of Charles was popular?

Source C

The execution of Charles I, from a contemporary print sold in Holland.

Questions

Section A

1 Copy the following paragraph, choosing one of the alternatives printed in *italics* each time.

When he was a prisoner in 1647 Charles *dealt fairly with/doubled crossed* the Army and the Presbyterians. He got the *Scots/Presbyterians* to start another war, fighting on his side. After the *Royalists/New Model Army* lost the war Charles made a deal with the *Royalist/Presbyterians* called the Treaty of Newport. This *pleased/upset* the Army. Pride's Purge cleared the *Presbyterians/Royalists* out of Parliament. The *Rump/Army* then ordered the *trial/trial and execution* of Charles.

Section B

The Second Civil War
The Treaty of Newport
Pride's Purge
Charles found guilty by the High Court of Justice

2 Historians have suggested these were all **causes** of Charles I's execution. Do you agree? Explain your answer.

3 Some causes **make it possible** for something else to happen. These are called **enabling causes** because they **enable** something to happen. Which of the causes on the list is an enabling cause? Give reasons for your answer.

4 Are all the causes on the list equally important in explaining why Charles I was executed? Give reasons for your answer.

5 Suggest two other causes why Charles I was executed.

The Commonwealth

The King was dead. The Rump went further. On 17 March 1649 it abolished the monarchy. Kings, it said, were 'unnecessary, burdensome, and dangerous to the liberty, safety, and public interest of the people'. Instead the Rump set up the **Commonwealth**. This was a republic, a country without a monarch, with its rulers elected by at least some of the people. To start off with, the Rump would be the Commonwealth's Parliament. New elections were promised later.

The new Commonwealth had plenty of enemies. Ireland was in the hands of rebels who were both Catholic and Royalist. The Scots were not happy about having their King executed by the English. The English Royalists were determined that Prince Charles should succeed his father. Luckily the Commonwealth also had one great friend, the Army. General Fairfax soon retired, and **Oliver Cromwell** took over. In three years, the Army beat the Irish, the Scots and then the English Royalists.

Many people at the time thought that God had a hand in events. When a war was won, the winners often claimed they had won because God was on their side. They called this **God's providence**. Many of the soldiers of the Army – including Cromwell and most of the officers – were Puritans. They believed that the victories from Naseby onwards proved God was on their side. They expected the Rump to make England a more godly country according to Puritan ideas.

Source A

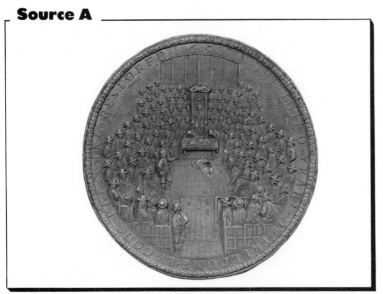

The Great Seal of the Commonwealth, 1651. The Seal shows the House of Commons.

1

The Army leaders were unhappy that there had been so little reform of the law. In December 1651, pressured by the Army (Colonel Pride stood by the door of the Commons, encouraging MPs), the Rump set up the **Hale Commission** to report on the changes needed in the law. The Commission made a report suggesting many changes to make the law fairer. The Rump ignored the report.

2

After the **Battle of Worcester**, Prince Charles escaped. He was helped to leave the country by a number of devoted Royalists.

3

In 1649 Cromwell went to **Ireland**. In a short but fierce campaign he defeated the rebels, leaving only small groups to be defeated and captured. After the siege of Drogheda Cromwell's soldiers killed almost all the defenders, even though many had surrendered. Cromwell said that in future the rebels would surrender before he attacked rather than when it was clear they had lost the battle. He also still blamed the Irish Catholics for the massacre of Protestants in 1641.

4

In 1651 war broke out against the **Dutch**. This war was mainly over who could trade where, and was fought at sea. It was very expensive, and not very popular. The Dutch were Protestants. Many people, especially Puritans, felt that all Protestant countries should stick together against the Catholic countries.

5

In 1650 the Scots invited Prince Charles to be their new king: **Charles II**. This was the start of a war with England. Cromwell invaded Scotland and at the **Battle of Dunbar** (3 September 1650) he destroyed the Scots army.

6

Puritans expected the Rump to improve the country's religion. They were worried that Catholicism and superstition were strong in some areas. The Rump set up the **Commission for the Propagation of the Gospel in Wales**. This paid for Puritan ministers to go and preach in Wales and try to convert people to their ideas. The Commission was a great success with the Puritans but less popular with the Rump. In 1653 it was thinking of stopping the grant which allowed the Commission to work.

7

In 1651 **Scots and English Royalists** combined to fight for Charles II. A joint army, led by Charles in person, got as far as Worcester. At **Worcester**, on 3 September 1651, Cromwell attacked and destroyed this army. He called the battle the 'crowning mercy'. Nobody in Britain was strong enough to threaten the Rump.

Source B

Act of Parliament, 1652.

Source C

Print from the title page of a pamphlet, 'The Vindication (Defence) of Christmas', 1653.

Questions

Section A

1 a What do the words say around the edge of the Great Seal?
  b What does this tell you about the Commonwealth?

2 Christmas was a holiday until the Rump changed the law. There was usually a great deal of feasting and merry-making. The Puritans thought that it was superstitions to celebrate Christmas.

  a Would Source B have pleased the Puritans in the Army?
  b Would Source B have pleased most ordinary people?
  c Do your answers to questions **2a** and **2b** suggest that there was a problem for the Rump?

3 Who are the two men on the left in Source C meant to be? Give reasons for your answer.

Section B

4 a Draw a time-line of the events from 1649 to 1653.
  b Divide your time-line into two sections: *The Rump threatened* and *The Rump safe*. Explain why you made the division at the point you chose.

5 Write a short essay on 'The Problems of the Rump Parliament'. You could write a paragraph about each of the following things: problems with the Irish, the Scots, the Royalists, the Dutch, and Cromwell and the Army. Write a conclusion where you say which you think were the most important problems and why.

39

Levellers and Diggers

The **Levellers** were an important group between 1647 and 1649. They had many supporters in the Army and in London. They wanted England to be a more democratic country. The story of one of their leaders, **John Lilburne**, shows the injustice they were fighting. They believed that the government would be truly fair only when their proposals for elections and laws were accepted.

John Lilburne

In 1637 he had been involved in smuggling into the country a book criticising Archbishop Laud. The authors had their ears cut off (see page 21). Lilburne was publicly whipped through the streets of London. After that he was kept in prison until the Long Parliament had him released in 1641. During the war he fought on Parliament's side. He got involved in quarrels with his general (the Earl of Manchester) and left the Army in 1644. In 1646 he was imprisoned by order of the House of Lords. He was released in 1647, winning a court case in which he claimed the House of Lords could not imprison him without a trial. In 1647 and 1648 he wrote many of the Levellers' books and petitions.

Lilburne argued for much more democracy and for freedom from arrest and imprisonment without a proper trial. In 1649 he was soon unhappy with the government of the Rump and campaigned against it. He was tried for treason but the jury found him innocent. Lilburne again upset the Rump when, in 1651, he quarrelled with one of its members. This time the Rump did not risk a jury trial but sentenced Lilburne itself. He was fined £8,000 and banished for life. He returned in 1653, saying that his banishment was illegal. He was tried in a proper court and found innocent. However, he was arrested immediately and imprisoned for the rest of his life.

The decline of the Levellers

The Levellers never really did agree about just who should have the vote. Most of them probably thought that servants should not be able to vote because a servant living in his master's house would be scared and vote the way his master told him. Elections for Parliament did not have a secret ballot. By 1649 they were losing their support in the Army. An attempt to start a mutiny failed when Cromwell smashed the mutineers at Burford. Without support in the Army the Levellers did not have the power to change things.

Lilburne being flogged in London, from a Dutch Print, about 1637.

Lilburne, from the front page of a book, 1646.

Lilburne pleading at his trial, a print, 1649

The Diggers

The **Diggers** sometimes called themselves **True Levellers**. They believed that to make society fair everybody needed to be free and equal. They thought this could not happen when some were very rich and others were very poor. They saw the problems as **land** and **wages**. England had many landowners. Some just owned the land they farmed, but others owned vast estates. The Diggers' solution was to confiscate all the land. Each person would then be given as much land as they could farm themselves, and working for wages would be made illegal. Nobody would take more land than they could farm themselves, because, without labourers to work it, it would be useless.

In April 1649 **Gerrard Winstanley** and a group of Diggers started to put this into practice. They moved on to some common land at **St George's Hill** in Surrey and started their own community. This alarmed the local landowners, who kept trying to have the community broken up. At first, General Fairfax refused, because he thought the Diggers were doing no harm. However, in 1650 the landowners succeeded. The Diggers' houses were burnt, their crops destroyed, and the people driven from the hill. Guards were posted to stop them coming back.

The Diggers were probably less likely to succeed than the Levellers. They did not have support in the Army or in London. However, many people at the time saw them as a greater threat. The poor would have had nothing to lose from the Diggers scheme, but much to gain. Because there were more poor people than rich people, the rich were worried about what might happen if the idea caught on.

Source D

'Parson Platt and others have informed you than we, called Diggers, are riotous, will not be ruled by justices, have seized a house and put 4 guns into it, and are cavaliers waiting an opportunity to rise. On which you sent soldiers to beat us. These reports are untrue. We are peaceable men, do not resist our enemies, and desire to conquer them by love.

We plough and dig so that the poor may get a living. We think we have a right to it because of the conquest over the late King.

We joined Parliament relying on promises of freedom of land. They said: "Give us your taxes, and adventure your lives with us. Cast out the oppressor Charles, and we will make you free people." Therefore we claim the freedom to enjoy the Common Lands, bought by our money and blood.'

From a letter by the Diggers to the Rump, 1649 or 1650.

Source E

A Digger pleading with General Fairfax. From the front page of a Digger book, 1649.

Questions

Section A

1 Draw a time-line of John Lilburne's life. He was born in 1615 and died in 1657. Shade in the time he spent in prison.

2 Do you think Sources A, B and C are sympathetic towards John Lilburne? Give reasons for your answer for each source.

3 Why did the Levellers not want to give the vote to every man?

4 How did the Diggers plan to make sure all people were equal?

Section B

5 In the seventeenth century women were traditionally seen as less important than men. It was also traditional for all men to wear hats, but to take them off when they were with their social superiors. How do you think Fairfax felt about the Diggers in Source E?

6 Do you think Lilburne would have approved of the trial and execution of Charles I?

7 Why do you think the Diggers called themselves 'True Levellers'?

41

Fifth Monarchists and Ranters

The **Fifth Monarchists** were an important religious and political group. You have met most of their main ideas before. They believed in the **Apocalypse** and the **Millennium** (see pages 6–7). They also believed that events since 1640 showed that God was against Charles I and on the side of reform (see pages 38–9). The Fifth Monarchists just took these ideas a little further.

The Bible prophecies about Antichrist and the end of the world talk about five monarchies. The first four were to be things like the Roman Empire. The fifth was to be a monarchy of Christ during which he would rule for 1,000 years with his saints. Most Puritans, indeed most Christians, believed this in England in the 1640s. The Fifth Monarchists went further. They believed that Christ would return and start the Fifth Monarchy as soon as people started to make godly reforms. They wanted to scrap the entire law of England and replace it with the laws of Moses from the Bible.

The Fifth Monarchists were happy at the execution of Charles I. This was part of the reform they needed to start a new monarchy, with King Jesus. They were not very interested in democracy; instead they wanted a government that did things according to their ideas. They had a lot of support in the Army and quite a bit in London.

Ranters also shared some of the beliefs you have read about earlier, especially **predestination** (see pages 6–7). While Cromwell and other powerful men had some sympathy for the Fifth Monarchists, there was little sympathy for the Ranters.

The Ranters believed that whether someone would go to heaven or hell (they said 'be saved' or 'dammed') was known by God before the person lived their life. They also believed that God would tell people whether they were going to be saved or damned. Most Puritans believed this. The Ranters took the idea to its illogical conclusion. What happened if one of the 'saved' committed a sin? It couldn't really be a sin because the person was going to be saved. Therefore the person had turned 'sin' into 'no-sin'. This must be a very godly thing to do. So the more 'sins' they committed, the more godly they were.

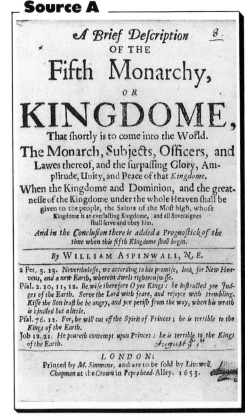

Part of the title page of a Fifth Monarchist book, 1653.

'Thus saith the Lord, *I inform you that I overturn, overturn, overturn*. And as the Bishops, Charles, and the Lords have had their turn, so your turn shall be next, ye surviving great ones. By what name or title, however dignified or distinguished, who ever you are that oppose me, the Eternal God, who am UNIVERSAL Love, and whose service is perfect freedom, and pure Libertinism.'

The first paragraph of 'The Fiery Flying Roll', a Ranter book published in 1649.

Their enemies (and they had plenty) described Ranter meetings as orgies. Puritans thought swearing and smoking were sins, so Ranters swore and smoked all the time. They also had sex with lots of people. It is not easy to decide what the Ranters believed. There are confessions from ex-Ranters, who accept the charges of sex, swearing and smoking tobacco. There are also one or two books written by Ranters trying to convert other people to Ranterism.

The Rump was horrified by the Ranters. A new Act of Parliament, the **Blasphemy Act**, was passed. This made sure that freedom to worship God in your own way did not apply to Ranters. They were persecuted and stamped out.

Questions

Section A

1 What beliefs did Fifth Monarchists share with most other Puritans?

2 What beliefs made Fifth Monarchists different from most other Puritans?

3 What beliefs did Ranters share with most other Puritans?

4 What beliefs made Ranters different from most other Puritans?

5 Sources B and C both come from the same book. What ideas do they share?

6 Does Source D give the same impression of the Ranters as Sources B and C? Explain your answer.

7 Do you think Source D was written by a Ranter or an anti-Ranter?

Section B

8 a How do you think a Ranter would have felt about the Diggers?

   b How do you think a Digger would have felt about the Ranters?

9 Would a Fifth Monarchist have approved of the abolition of the monarchy by the Rump after the execution of Charles I?

10 How do you think Oliver Cromwell, who was a Puritan and a soldier, felt about:

   a The Fifth Monarchists?
   b The Ranters?

11 What would a Ranter have thought about getting drunk on a Sunday?

12 What would a Fifth Monarchist have thought about getting drunk on a Sunday?

Source C

A Fiery Flying Roll : 13

A

Word from the Lord to all the Great Ones of the Earth, whom this may concerne : Being the last WARNING PIECE at the dreadfull day of JUDGEMENT.

For now the LORD is come

to { 1 Informe
     2 Advise and warne } the Great Ones.
     3 Charge
     4 Judge and sentence

As also most compassionately informing, and most lovingly and pathetically advising and warning London.

With a terrible Word, and fatall Blow from the Lord, upon the Gathered CHURCHES.

And all by his Most Excellent MAJESTY, dwelling in, and shining through AUXILIUM PATRIS, alias, Coppe..

With another FLYING ROLL ensuing (to all the Inhabitants of the Earth.) The Contents of both following.

Isa. 23. 9, The Lord of Hosts (is) staining the pride of all glory, and bringing into contempt all the honourable (persons and things) of the Earth.
O London, London, how would I gather thee, as a hen gathereth her chickens under her Wings, &c.
Know then (in this thy day) the things that belong to thy Peace——
I know the blasphemy of them which say they are Jewes, and are not, but are the Synagogue of Satan, Rev. 2. 9.   Jan. 4. 1649

Imprinted at London, in the beginning of that notable day, wherein the secrets of all hearts are laid open; and wherein the worst and foulest of villanies, are discovered, under the best and fairest outsides. 1649.

Title page of 'The Fiery Flying Roll', 1649.

Source D

The Ranters Declaration,

WITH

Their new Oath and Protestation; their strange Votes, and a new way to get money; their Proclamation and Summons; their new way of Ranting, never before heard of; their dancing of the Hey naked, at the white Lyon in Peticoat-lane; their mad Dream, and Dr. Pockridge his Speech, with their Trial, Examination, and Answers: the coming in of 3000. their Prayer and Recantation, to be in all Cities and Market-towns read and published; the mad-Ranters further Resolution; their Christmas Carol, and blaspheming Song; their two pretended-abominable Keyes to enter Heaven, and the worshiping of his little majesty, the late Bishop of Canterbury: A new and further Discovery of their black Art, with the Names of those that are possest by the Devil, having strange and hideous cries heard within them, to the great admiration of all those that shall read and peruse this ensuing subject.

Licensed according to order, and published by M. Stubs, a late fellow-Ranter.

Title page of 'The Ranter's Declaration', 1650.

43

Witchcraft

During the sixteenth and seventeenth centuries **witches** were persecuted all over Europe. In England suspected witches were not tortured, and convicted witches were hanged not burnt. In Scotland both torture and burning were used, and there were many more trials and executions.

The only time when there were mass **witch-hunts** in England was just after the Civil War. This was the only time when there were professional witch-hunters in England. The witch-hunter mentioned in Source E was paid £1 for every witch he discovered. The most famous English witch-hunter was **Matthew Hopkins**, who worked in the eastern counties. Between 1645 and 1647 he was probably responsible for the conviction of 200 people as witches.

You have seen how most people in Britain believed that God was actively involved in what happened in their world. They also believed that the Devil was active, working against God. A monstrous birth, such as that mentioned in Source B, was taken as a warning from God that something was wrong. If beer went sour or a cow fell sick, it made as much sense to most people to look for a

---

Source A

Proof that somebody is a witch

'1 The common report of the greater sort of people with whom the person suspected lives, that he or she is a witch.
2 If a fellow witch gives testimony that a person is a witch.
3 If, after cursing, there follows death, or at least some mischief.
4 If after quarrelling or threatening, a mischief does follow.
5 If the person suspected be the son or daughter, the manservant or maidservant, the familiar friend or near neighbour of a witch.
6 If the person suspected be found to have the Devil's mark.
7 If the person, being examined, contradicts in their answers.'

From William Perkins, 'A Discourse on the Damned Art of Witchcraft', 1608.

Source B

Signes and wonders from Heaven. 2

With a true Relation of a Monster borne in *Ratcliffe High-way*, at the signe of the three Arrows, Mistris *Bullock* the Midwife delivering her thereof.

Also shewing how a Cat kitned a Monster in *Lombardstreet* in *London*.

Likewise a new discovery of Witches in *Stepney* Parish. And how 20. Witches more were executed in *Suffolke* this last Assise. Also how the Divell came to Soffam to a Farmers house in the habit of a Gentlewoman on horse-backe.

With divers other strange remarkible passages.

Aug: 5   Printed at *London* by *I. H.*

A pamphlet from the 1640s.

Source C

Witches Apprehended, Examined and Executed, for notable villanies by them committed both by Land and Water.

With a strange and most true triall how to know whether a woman be a Witch or not.

Title page of a book on witchcraft.

supernatural explanation as to look for a natural one. Witches were thought to be people who made a contract with the Devil. The Devil would give them powers during their life, in return for their soul when they died. Usually they were given **familiars**, evil spirits that often took the shape of small animals.

Most witches in England were accused of using their powers to cause damage or **maleficium**. Usually it was something like making a cow sick, making beer go sour in the barrel or stopping milk from churning into butter. Sometimes the maleficium was more deadly, such as killing farm animals, or injuring or even killing humans.

Not all court records survive from the sixteenth and seventeenth centuries, but historians have studied most that have. People accused of being witches have a number of things in common. They were usually poor and quite old, mostly aged over 40. Nine out of ten were women, and many of them were widows. They were often people who would have to ask for charity from their neighbours to help them live.

Source F

Matthew Hopkins examining a witch about her familiars, from the title page of a book, 1647.

Source D

'Every old woman with a wrinkled face, a furr'd brow, a hairy lip, a gobber tooth, a squint eye, a squeaking voice, or a scolding tongue is pronounced a witch.'

Reverend John Gaule, 1646.

Source E

A witch hunter in Newcastle upon Tyne, 1649

'The witch finder told Lieutenant Colonel Hobson that he knew whether women were witches or not by their looks. When the witch finder was searching a good looking woman, the Colonel replied and said, "Surely this woman is none, and need not be tested." But the Scotsman said she was, because people in the town said she was, and therefore he would test her. In the sight of all the people he laid her body naked to the waist, with her clothes over her head. With fright and shame all the blood contracted to one part of her body. And then he ran a pin into her thigh, and suddenly let her clothes fall, and asked why she did not bleed. Then he put his hand up her clothes and took out the pin and set her aside as a guilty person and child of the Devil. Lieutenant Colonel Hobson, having seen the way the woman's blood settled, caused the woman to be brought again, and her clothes pulled up to her thigh. He required the witch finder to run the pin into the same place, and then blood gushed out, and the witch finder cleared her and said she was not a child of the devil.'

Questions

Section A

1 Copy out the following paragraph, choosing one of the alternatives printed in *italics* each time.

More/fewer witches were persecuted in England than in Europe. In England witches *were/were* not tortured and, if they were found guilty, they were *hanged/burnt*. People accused of witchcraft had usually committed crimes such as *turning beer sour/flying on a broomstick*. Most were women and they were usually *over/under* 40. *Matthew Hopkins/Lieutenant Colonel Hobson* was a professional witch-hunter, but they were rare.

2 List the 'proofs' that someone was a witch. For each one, say whether you think it is a convincing proof.

Section B

3 Some people confessed to being witches, knowing the punishment was death. Why did they do this?

4 Would people at the time have linked the monstrous birth and the discovery of witches (Source B)?

The Protectorate

Cromwell dismisses the Rump Parliament, from a print sold at the time.

End of the Rump Parliament

The failure of the Rump to make the sort of reforms which the Army and its supporters wanted proved fatal. In April 1653 the Rump was even discussing a new scheme for elections in which existing members of the Rump would not need to be re-elected. This was too much for Cromwell. He believed that the leaders of the Rump had agreed to new elections in a meeting with him the day before. He took soldiers with him and went to the House. After listening to the debate for a while he stood up in a rage and told the Rump: 'You have sat here long enough.' He called his soldiers in and cleared the House.

Barebone's Parliament

Cromwell and the Army did not want to turn the country into a military dictatorship – after all, they had been fighting for freedom. On the other hand, they could not be sure that elections would choose MPs with the same ideas as they had. They set up a Parliament where the members were nominated rather than elected. Cromwell and his advisers had the final say about who would sit, but they asked for suggestions from churches and other groups around the country. This Parliament first met on 4 July 1653. It is called **Barebone's Parliament** after one of its members, Praise-God Barebone.

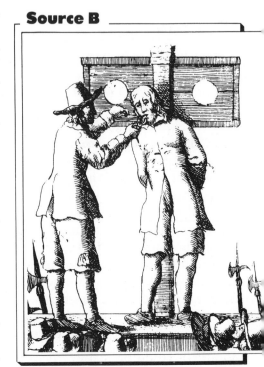

Part of the punishment of James Nayler, from a print sold at the time.

Some Fifth Monarchists were members of Barebone's Parliament. There were also plenty of moderate gentlemen, from the families whose men traditionally became MPs. The Fifth Monarchists were careful to go to every debate and they often won the votes even though most MPs were not Fifth Monarchists. Worried by this the moderate MPs all turned up early on 12 December 1653. They resigned and gave power back to Cromwell.

The Protectorate

For the second time in a year Cromwell found himself with total power over Britain. He set up a government with a **constitution**, a law which said exactly what the government's power was. The Protectorate was more like the old monarchy. At the head of government was the **Protector** (Cromwell himself). The Protector had the sort of power the Long Parliament had wanted to leave Charles. There was also to be a Parliament, at least once every three years. Ex-Royalists were banned from voting, to make sure that Parliament had the right sort of ideas.

The Parliaments found plenty to criticise. The first one, in 1654, tried to change the constitution. Cromwell did not agree and eventually dismissed the Parliament. The second Parliament, in 1656, wanted Cromwell to become King. He refused. While many people in the country wanted to get back to the old ways and liked the idea of having a king, Cromwell and many of the Army could not forget that they had fought wars to stop England having one.

The case of James Nayler

The Parliament of 1656 also quarrelled with Cromwell about **James Nayler**. Nayler had re-enacted Christ's entry into Jerusalem on Palm Sunday. In Nayler's case he entered Bristol, with women strewing the ground in front of him with leaves and clothes. This was seen as **blasphemy**. Parliament was horrified. It decided that Nayler ought to be punished and had him brought to London. Parliament made itself accuser, judge and jury. It found Nayler guilty and discussed the death penalty. Finally it decided on a 'milder' punishment. Nayler was to be put in the pillory and be publicly whipped, have his tongue bored through with a red-hot iron, be branded with a 'B' (for blasphemer) on the forehead, be taken to Bristol, publicly whipped again, returned to London and kept in prison until Parliament decided to let him out.

To Cromwell this did not look much like the freedom and liberty he had spent the last fifteen years fighting for. Parliament could be just as much a tyrant as Charles had been. The constitution had limited his powers as Protector but it had not limited the power of Parliament enough.

Questions

Section A

1 Who do you think the following people in Source A are:

2 Most of the MPs who sentenced Nayler were sincere Christians who did not believe they were being cruel. How can this be explained?

3 Why do you think people bought prints of Nayler's punishments?

Section B

4 Write out these lists in their correct **chronological order**.

   a Nayler sentenced; James Nayler entered Bristol; Nayler bored through the tongue; Parliament sent for Nayler.

   b Parliament of 1656, Rump Parliament dismissed; Barebone's Parliament first met; Protectorate set up.

   c Charles I became king; Oliver Cromwell died; first Civil War; Protectorate set up.

5 Some historians have said that Cromwell was ambitious and power hungry. Others have said he was not. Use the information in this unit to answer the question: *Was Cromwell after power for himself?* Try to give some reasons which would support the answer 'yes' and some which would support the answer 'no'. Then come to a conclusion; say what you think the answer is and why you have chosen that answer.

47

Oliver Cromwell

A Royalist print showing Cromwell and his advisers.

Oliver Cromwell is an important figure in the history of Britain. He is also a man historians have often disagreed about. The disagreement is not about **what** he did but about **why** he did it. This is not, however, why he is important. He is important because of the **effect** he had on Britain. The past would have been different if Cromwell had not lived.

Cromwell was one of the first soldiers to see that Parliament's armies were not good enough at the start of the Civil War. His own troops were among the best on either side. In 1644 he was one of the leaders of the criticism of the way Parliament was fighting the war. The **New Model Army** was the result of these debates.

In 1647 Cromwell faced an agonising choice. He had to support either Parliament or the Army. In the end he chose the Army. Because the Army survived it was able to press Parliament not to make a deal with Charles I. The Army was also there to win the **Second Civil War** in 1648. Once the war was won, Cromwell was one of the leaders in the movement to have Charles I tried and executed.

Between 1649 and 1653 Cromwell the soldier was as important as Cromwell the politician. He virtually conquered Ireland in 1649. In 1650, when General Fairfax would not fight against the Scots, he took over command of the Army. In two years he beat the Scots and the English Royalists and also conquered Scotland.

Source A

Painting of Cromwell done in the late 1640s. Cromwell is said to have told an artist starting a portrait of him: 'I desire you would use all your skill to paint my picture truly like me, and not flatter me at all; but remark all these roughnesses, pimples, warts and everything as you see me, otherwise I will never pay a farthing for it.'

For the rest of his life Cromwell was a politician rather than a soldier. He kept the Army loyal to the Rump long after most soldiers lost faith in it. Finally he also ran out of patience and expelled the Rump. Rather than take all power for himself, he first set up Barebone's Parliament and, when that failed, the Protectorate. As **Lord Protector** he liked to be treated almost like a king, but he refused the crown when it was offered.

Questions

1 Draw a time-line showing the main events of Oliver Cromwell's life. These dates will help: born 1599; died 1658; married 1620; MP 1628–9; MP in Short Parliament 1640; MP in Long Parliament; children born 1621, 1623, 1624, 1626, 1628, 1629, 1637, 1638; death of children 1639, 1644, 1658.

2 Does Cromwell's life divide into neat sections? If so, what are they?

3 Copy and complete the table below showing some of the main decisions of Cromwell's life. In the 'effect' column try to think what might have happened if he had not made the choice he did.

4 Having thought more about Cromwell, would you change your answer to question 5 in Unit 1.23? Explain your answer.

Date	Event or problem	Cromwell's action	Effect
1640	Whether to support or oppose Charles I in Parliament	Supported John Pym in his attacks on Charles. Not a very important MP at this stage	
1642	Whether to fight for Parliament in the Civil War	Formed a troop of cavalry in the Civil War which was successful and grew into a regiment	
1644	What to do about Parliament's failure to win the war	Led criticism of the generals – especially Manchester and Essex. Supported the creation of the New Model Army in Parliament and the resignation of all old commanders	
1647	Whether to support the Army or Parliament	Supported the Army against Parliament. Helped stop the Levellers' attempt to take over the Army	
1648–9	What to do about Charles I after the Second Civil War	Helped force through the trial and execution of Charles	
1649	Campaign in Ireland	Irish rebels defeated, although with some charges of cruelty	
1650	Threat from Scotland	Invaded Scotland, beat Scots at Battle of Dunbar	
1651	Threat from Scots and English Royalists	Combined armies defeated at Battle of Worcester	
1653	What to do about the Rump	Used soldiers to expel the Rump and set up Barebone's Parliament	
1653–4	What to do after Barebone's Parliament resigned.	Set up Protectorate	
1657	Asked to become King by Parliament.	Refused	

The Restoration

Source A

'Next morning the Council ordered the proclamation of Richard (Cromwell as Lord Protector) to be made at ten o'clock at Whitehall. The proclamation was followed by loud cries of "God Save the Lord Protector" and great applause at Whitehall, Westminster, Temple Bar, Cheapside and the Royal Exchange in Cornhill. In Exeter, on 6 September, the magistrates and Council proclaimed Richard. When this had been done the crowd shouted, "Amen, amen, God preserve my Lord Richard Lord Protector". The proclamation caused equal enthusiasm throughout England. Sometimes wine and beer were distributed free; sometimes volleys of shots, the ringing of bells, bonfires and "treats" were features of the celebrations.

Godfrey Davies, 'The Restoration of Charles II', 1955.

Source B

The return of Charles II in 1660.
'He arrived at Dover about 2 o'clock in the afternoon. Ready on the shore to receive him stood the Lord General Monk, the Constable of Dover Castle, many persons of quality and the mayor of Dover. From there he went to Barham Down, where multitudes of the country people stood, making loud shouts. He rode to the head of each group of them, who, bowing to him, kissed the hilts of their swords then waved them above their heads, with no less shouting. At Canterbury the mayor and aldermen received him with loud music, and presented him with a cup of gold, worth £250. In magnificent fashion his majesty entered the city of London at the Bridge; where he found the windows and streets exceedingly thronged with people to see him. The walls decorated with hangings of tapestry and other costly stuff. All the fountains, as he passed, running claret wine.'

From 'England's Joy', 1660.

Oliver Cromwell died on 3 September 1658. He was succeeded by his son, Richard. Source A shows how popular this was. Oliver was given an expensive state funeral in Westminster Abbey. Less than two years later, **Charles II** was welcomed by enthusiastic crowds (Source B). Oliver Cromwell's body was dug up and taken to Tyburn. (This was where public hangings took place.) Also taken were the bodies of Ireton (his son-in-law) and Bradshaw (the judge at Charles I's trial). The bodies were hanged. After a couple of hours they were taken down and beheaded. The rest of the bodies were thrown into an unmarked pit. The heads were stuck on spikes outside Whitehall. They stayed there until they were blown down in a gale, some twenty years later. What had happened to change so much so quickly?

The English Revolution had collapsed. Richard Cromwell had not been able to control the Army. He soon resigned and was replaced by the Rump Parliament. The Rump and the Army still could not agree. In quick succession the Army expelled the Rump again, and then accepted it back. Most people were unhappy at all the

Questions

Section A

1 Write out these lists in their correct **chronological order**.

   a Monk marched to London; Oliver Cromwell died; Rump Parliament restored; Declaration of Breda.

   b Richard Cromwell proclaimed Protector in Exeter; Richard Cromwell resigned from the Protectorship; Richard Cromwell proclaimed Protector in London; Oliver Cromwell died.

2 For each of Sources A, B and C say whether the source is primary or secondary. Give reasons for your answer in each case.

3 Why do you think Cromwell, Ireton and Bradshaw's bodies were punished?

Source C

Vengeance of the Royalists. The bodies of Cromwell, Ireton and Bradshaw hanged and beheaded.

Section B

4 a Did the Army in London want Charles II back?

  b Did the London Army's actions help cause the Restoration?

5 Was the Declaration of Breda likely to help Charles II get back the throne?

6 Was the loyalty of Monk's soldiers to him a cause of the Restoration?

7 Make up your own cause-and-effect diagram for the Restoration. Use the following labels for the boxes:

Army not willing to accept government it didn't like; Army became more unpopular; Charles II popular; Monk wanted strong and fair government; Declaration of Breda.

Use arrows and shade boxes to show causes and effects. Some labels might be both.

changes. They wanted a strong and fair government. After Oliver's death nobody seemed able to supply one.

Eventually **General Monk**, commander of the Army in Scotland, marched to London. He did not say what he would do when he got there. His part of the Army was probably the strongest and it was loyal to him. The Army in England was split with quarrels about politics and religion. When Monk arrived in London he decided to restore the Long Parliament. This meant getting back as many of the original MPs of 1640 as were still around. Ex-Royalists came back to the Commons, as did the Presbyterians kept out by Pride's Purge in 1648. Monk knew that a House of Commons with these men in it would try to restore Charles I's son.

There were still big problems to be solved before Charles II could return. The main questions were:

- What would happen about the Church? Would the Church of England be the only one allowed, or would Puritans still be allowed to set up their own churches?
- What would happen to all the people who had fought against Charles I? Would they be punished?
- What would happen to all the land which had been confiscated from Royalists and from the King? Much of it had been sold to raise money.
- Would the soldiers get the pay that they were still owed?

Charles's answer to these problems was the **Declaration of Breda**. In it he said he would accept Parliament's suggestions about all four problems.

Mr Pepys

Samuel Pepys was not a famous man while he was alive. He was a civil servant, working for the navy. He is famous because, between 1660 and 1669, he kept a diary. Written in shorthand, partly to save time and partly to be sure his wife could not read it, **Pepys's Diary** describes his life in considerable detail. We learn about the ordinary things of everyday life. This is often hard information for historians to find.

There are many famous entries in Pepys's Diary. He crossed the Channel with Charles II when the King returned to England in 1660. He was in London during the **Great Plague** and the **Great Fire**. This unit avoids the famous entries, however. It tries to give an idea of what Pepys's life was like by looking at what he did on the same day each year.

'16 April 1660. (Pepys was with the fleet which had gone to bring Charles II to England). About 4 o'clock in the morning Mr Cooke waked me in the Great Cabin, and I gave him the letters for London. So to sleep again. All morning giving out orders to the commanders of the fleet. After dinner busy all the afternoon writing – and so till night; then to bed.'

'16 April 1661. As soon as word was brought to me that Mr Coventry was come with the barge to the Tower, I went to him. Here he and I sat till the Comptroller came; and then we put off for Deptford, where we went on board the King's pleasure boat that Commissioner Pett is making. From there to Commissioner Pett's lodging and there had a good breakfast. And so we sat down and did a great deal of business about fitting out the fleet.

That done we went to the Globe and there had a good dinner. And by and by took barge again and so home. By the way they would have me sing, which I did, and we stayed and talked a good while and then broke up. And I home and then to my father's and there I slept with my wife.'

'16 April 1662. Up early and took my medicine, it worked well all through the morning. At noon dined, and all the afternoon, with Mr Hater, he and I did check all the contracts made in the office since we came into it. So at night to bed.'

'16 April 1663. Up betimes and to my office. Later met to check Mr Pitt's accounts for the voyage to the Straits (of Gibraltar). They are strangely irregular, but I dare not oppose them alone, in case I make an enemy. At noon home for an hour to dinner, and so to the office, till late at night, so home to supper and bed, my father with us.'

'16 April 1664. Up and to the office all morning. At noon with Mr Coventry to the African-house. And after a good and pleasant dinner, with him to check my Lord Peterborough's accounts, but the more we look into them the more we see of them that makes dispute. So I home and there to find my wife and Bess (her maid) gone over the water to Halfwayhouse; and I after them thinking to have gone to Woolwich, but it was too late. So eat a cake and home, and then by coach to have spoke with Tom Trice about a letter I had this afternoon. But I find him gone out of town and so returned cross home and then to the office, where late writing a letter to him. And so home to bed.'

'16 April 1665. Lord's day. Lay long in bed. Then up and to my chamber and my office, looking over some plans, which I need to understand well because of the Dutch War. Then home to dinner, where Creed dined with us. After dinner he and I walked to the Rolls chapel expecting to hear the great Stillingfleet preach; but he did not, but a very sorry fellow, which vexed me. The sermon done we parted and I came home, where I find Mr Andrews and Captain Taylor that understands music so well. He brought us some things to sing – very hard. He supped with me, and a good understanding man is he and a good scholar. He gone, we to bed. This night I am told that news is come of our taking three Dutch men-of-war, with the loss of one of our captains.'

'16 April 1666. Up, and set my people, Mercer, Hewer, Tom and the girl, to work ruling and stitching ruled books for the Muster Masters. I hard at work on my Tangier accounts. At noon dined alone, the girl Mercer taking medicine can eat nothing, and Hewer went out to dinner. So up to my accounts again. Then comes Mrs Mercer and fair Mrs Turner, a neighbour of hers my wife knows. I stayed a great while with them, being taken with this pretty woman – though a mighty silly affected woman she is. I left them, to come back at supper, and went by coach to an old woman in Pannyer Alley for some ruled papers, and they are done. And I am much more taken with her dark haired maid, Nan. So home and there came Mrs Turner and Mercer and supped with me, and well pleased I was with their company, especially Mrs Turner's, she being a very pretty woman. They stayed with me talking until about 11 o'clock, and then home and so I to bed.'

'16 April 1667. Up, and to the office, where sat all the morning. At noon home to dinner, and then in haste to take my wife to see the play I saw yesterday, she not knowing it. But there, not what I expected, I find The Silent Woman. Knipp tells me the King was so angry at the play yesterday, that he commanded they should act no more. Moore went to see him and got leave they should act again, but not that play. Thence with my wife and Knipp to Mrs Pierce's. Thence took them all to the Cake House. They talk of yesterday's play and I dare not admit to my wife I have seen it. Thence home to look on my new books that I have lately bought; and then to supper and to bed.'

'16 April 1668. Began this day to learn the recorder. To the office all morning. Dined with my clerks. To Whitehall by coach to the Commissioners of the Treasury, but they met not. To Westminster by water (6 pence). There spoke with many. Thence to Whitehall, but no meeting of the Commissioners. Thence to Mrs Martin and there did what I would, she troubled for want of employment for her husband. Spent on her one shilling. Thence to the Hall to walk a while. Spent on a ribbon one shilling. So to Lord Crew's and there talk. So to the Temple late and by water by moonlight home (1 shilling). Displeased to find my maid bring her brother, a countryman, to lie the night. So to bed.'

Questions

1 Copy out the following table. Fill it in as you read through each entry in the Diary. Note down the useful information you get from the Diary about each topic and the date of the entry where you found it.

Topic	Evidence from the Diary
Transport	
Meals a What meals were called b When each meal was eaten c Where meals were eaten	
Work a How regularly does Pepys go to work? b What hours does he work?	
Leisure a What does Pepys do in his spare time? b What time was the theatre performance?	

2 Copy each of the following sentences, into your book, underline it and say whether you think the Diary proves it is true, suggests it might be true, suggests it might not be true, or proves it is not true. In each case give reasons for your answer.
   a Pepys was not married.
   b Pepys sometimes worked on accounts.
   c Pepys was a very religious man.
   d Women lived a fairly free life in London at the time.
   e Pepys was a hard-working man.
   f London was a violent city at the time.

3 Pepys seems to have kept his Diary a secret. Nobody knew about it for over 100 years after his death. Does this make it more or less valuable for historians?

4 If you wrote a diary, how might it be valuable to historians in later years?

The Plague

Plague struck London a number of times during the seventeenth century. By far the worst was the **Great Plague** of 1665.

Doctors did not know what caused the Plague. Some thought it was caused by the position of the planets. Most thought it was caught from bad smells or touch. There were plenty of bad smells in London. Often the plague was thought to be a punishment from God. People could think this and also think that it was spread by bad smells.

There were no really successful treatments for the Plague. Isolation was the main one, shutting the sick up until they either died or got better. This didn't really help the sick people but it was felt that it would stop them spreading the Plague to others. Those who could afford to left London, only returning when the weekly **Bills of Mortality** (which listed the dead and what they died from) showed that the Plague was more or less over. Those who stayed in London were worried about touching things which might have been touched by the sick.

Shopkeepers kept dishes of vinegar on their counters. They would not take money from their customers, it was dropped in the vinegar and then picked up by the shopkeeper. Shoppers would pick up what they wanted themselves, not be handed things by the shopkeeper. Most people carried 'posies' – sweet-smelling herbs and flowers. If they could not afford posies they carried cloth soaked in vinegar.

Source A

London's Bill of Mortality for 1665.

Source B

Orders of the Lord Mayor of London concerning the Plague, 1665

'*Examiners* to enquire what houses in every parish be Visited, what persons be sick, and of what diseases. If they find one sick of the Plague, to give order to the Constable that the house be shut up.

Searchers. Women-Searchers be sworn to make search and true report whether the persons do die of the Plague. No Searcher be permitted to keep any shop or stall, or be employed as a laundress.

Doctors to join with Searchers to view the body, that there may be a true report made of the disease.

Isolation of the Sick. As soon as any be found to be sick of the Plague, they shall be shut in their house, and the house shut for a month.

Burial of the Dead be always either before sun-rising or after sun-setting. No neighbours or friends be suffered to accompany the corpse to church, or enter the dead person's house, on pain of having their own house shut up. All graves shall be at least six foot deep.

Every Visited house to be marked with a red cross a foot long, in the middle of the door, and with these usual printed words, "Lord Have Mercy Upon Us".

Every Visited House to be watched by watchmen who shall get necessaries unto them.

The streets to be kept clean and the filth of houses be daily carried away. That no hogs, dogs, cats, tame pigeons or rabbits be kept within the city, or any pigs in the streets or lanes.'

Source C

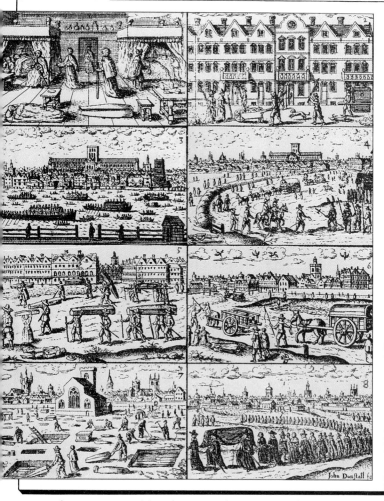

Scenes from a print sold at the time, showing London during the Plague.

Source D

'*7 June.* This day I did in Drury Lane see two or three houses marked with a red cross upon the doors and "Lord Have Mercy Upon Us" writ there. It put me into an ill conception of myself and my smell, so that I was forced to buy some roll tobacco to smell and chaw – which took away the worry.

10 June. Home to bed – being troubled at the sickness, and my head filled with business enough, particularly how to put my things and estate in good order, in case it should please God to call me away.

16 October. But Lord how empty the streets are, and melancholy, so many poor sick people in the streets, full of sores. Everybody talking of this dead and that man sick, and so many in this place and so many in that.'

Entries in Pepys's Diary during the summer of 1665.

Questions

Empathy

Section A

1 Copy out these sentences, choosing the correct 'tail' to go with each 'head'.

Heads	Tails
a Plague was a common problem	not touching things others had touched and carrying posies.
b Doctors did not know	by bad smells, others by touch.
c Some thought it was spread	to stop them spreading it.
d If people had the Plague they were shut up	in seventeenth-century London.
e People tried to avoid the Plague by leaving London,	what caused it.

2 a How many people died from the Plague in 1665?

   b How many died from it in 1664?

   c Does Source A suggest that medicine has improved since 1665?

3 a Why were the Searchers not allowed to have shops?
   b How did the Mayor think the Plague was spread?

4 Do Sources C and D suggest that historians can rely on Source B to tell them about London during the Plague?

Section B

5 Would people have thought that shutting the sick in houses was cruel?

6 Sniffing vinegar-soaked cloth would not stop a person catching the Plague. Why did people do it?

The Fire of London

Print of the Fire, 1666.

Source B

Engraving of the Fire, 1666.

Source D

'*2 September 1666.* Walked to the Tower and there got up on one of the high places. I did see the houses at that end of the bridge all on fire, and an infinite great fire on this and the other side of the end of the bridge. The Lieutenant of the Tower tells me it begun this morning in the King's-baker's house in Pudding Lane. Everybody trying to remove their goods, and flinging into the River or bringing them into boats. Poor people staying in their houses as long as till the very fire touched them, and then running into boats. I stayed, and in an hour's time saw the fire rage every way, and nobody to my sight trying to quench it, but to remove their goods and leave all to the fire. The wind mighty high and driving it into the city, and everything, after so long a drought, proving combustible. It being darkish we saw the fire as one entire arch of fire from this to the other side of the bridge. It made me weep to see it. The churches, houses and all on fire and flaming at once, and a horrid noise the flames made, and the cracking of houses at their ruin. So home with a sad heart.'

Samuel Pepys's Diary.

Source C

Print showing London in 1647.

Source E

Map showing London after the fire, 1666. The title of the map is: 'A map or groundplot of the city of London, with the suburbs thereof so far as the Lord Mayor's jurisdiction doth extend, by which is exactly demonstrated the present condition of it since its last sad accident of fire, the blank space signifying the burnt part and where the houses be those places yet standing.'

The strange case of Robert Hubert

The **Fire of London** was such a terrible disaster that many could not believe it was an accident. A Catholic plot was suspected. People fleeing from London spread the rumour. Catholics were set upon in the streets. One was nearly killed when a crowd thought he had 'balls of fire'. They turned out to be tennis balls. As far away as Warwick a suspicious man was seen near a 'blackish-brown ball'. Again balls of fire were suspected, and an angry mob set after the man. Henry Young, a distiller, claimed that a Jesuit had told him in 1661 that 'Within seven years all England would be Roman Catholic.' Young had replied that the City of London would never endure it. The Jesuit answered that 'Within five or six years they would break the power and strength of London in pieces'.

Robert Hubert, a Frenchman, who claimed to be a Roman Catholic, was arrested for starting the fire. He confessed and was able to show where the house the Fire started in had been. He was executed on 29 October. The only evidence against Hubert was his confession. The site of the house had been displayed for visitors as soon as the Fire was over. Historians think that Hubert was not in England until two days after the Fire started.

Questions

1 Do Sources A and B agree about where the Fire was?

2 Does Source C suggest that Sources A and B are reliable?

3 Which source is most useful for working out where the Fire was?

4 Which sources are most useful for working out how the Fire spread? Give reasons for your answer.

5 What other sources could you use to check where the Fire burnt?

6 Does Source D prove that:
   a Pepys was in London on the day the Fire started?
   b People tried to save their possessions?

7 a What evidence was there that Hubert started the Fire?
   b Do you think this evidence was good enough to be proof?

8 Is the story of Hubert reliable evidence about how many people felt about Roman Catholics?

King James II

During the last years of **Charles II's** reign, people worried about the **succession**. Charles had no legitimate children. This meant that the heir to the throne was Charles's brother, **James**. The problem was that James was a Roman Catholic. Catholics were still very unpopular with most English people. There was a campaign to stop James becoming the next King. However people could also remember the Civil Wars. They wanted to keep having kings in the traditional way. The supporters of James won. He was the proper heir to the throne. Also he had no son, and both his daughters were Protestants. There would be only a short period with a Catholic king.

Partly because people were glad that everything was settled without another war, James was very popular when he became King in 1685. Soon after he became King there was a rebellion against him. The **Duke of Monmouth**, a Protestant and an illegitimate son of Charles II, raised an army in the West. Monmouth did not get much support. His soldiers were mainly peasants with pitchforks and scythes rather than muskets and cannon. They were easily defeated at the **Battle of Sedgemore**. Monmouth was captured, tried and executed. Most people probably thought that this was fair. But they did not think that the persecution of Monmouth's followers was fair. King James sent **Judge Jeffries**, one of his strong supporters, to try the rebels. Over 500 were executed, and a further 800 were sold as slaves for ten years to plantations in the West Indies.

James II was determined to make **Catholicism** the most important religion in England. The first step was to allow Roman Catholics to be members of the government and officers in the army. There was a law which said that only members of the Church of England could be either of these things. James claimed the right to suspend any law if he wanted to. He suspended this one. He sacked most of the judges and appointed new ones who agreed with him. The judges said that James could suspend any law he liked.

The next step in James II's campaign was to get Catholics involved in local government. **Magistrates** who would not accept James's power to suspend laws were sacked and replaced by anyone who would. The Magistrates who were sacked were members of the **gentry**. They saw themselves as the proper people to run England. No king could afford to lose their support.

James became more and more unpopular. The final straw for many people was when he had a son in 1688. This boy would grow up a Roman Catholic. Because he was a boy he would be the next monarch, not James's eldest

Judge Jeffries.

William of Orange lands.

Questions

1 The frames of the cartoon can be rearranged to tell the story of James II. Copy them into your book in the right order, adding a sentence or two of your own to each caption to help explain the story.

2 Most of the political problems you have read about so far in this book have been about two things. People wanted to have real **freedom** and they were worried about how **religion** was organised. How would people have judged James on these two issues?

James gets a son.

James suspends anti-Catholic law

Many JPs sacked.

Monmouth's Rebellion.

James becomes king, 1685.

daughter. Rumours went round that the boy was not James's son. It was said a baby had been smuggled into the Queen's bedroom and then presented as the Queen's baby. The stories were almost certainly not true. Many people wanted to believe them, though.

James's eldest daughter, **Mary** was married to **William of Orange**, a Protestant Dutch prince. William had many supporters in England. Late in 1688 he was persuaded to oppose James. He issued a declaration saying that he wanted to protect his wife's rights and listing things James had done which were illegal. First on the list was the claim to suspend any law he wanted to. William also said that he would accept any settlement that Parliament made. He landed with an army in Torbay on 5 November. William slowly advanced on London. When James sent his army to stop the advance, most of the troops changed sides. James tried to flee the country but was caught by fishermen on the Isle of Sheppey and returned to London. This did not suit William, who did not want any question of executing a king to come up again. James was allowed to escape again. This time he got away to France.

3 When James claimed that he could suspend any law, it was like saying he could choose not to punish people. Why did so many other people see this as a threat to their liberty?

4 A courtier who knew both James II and Charles II said: 'Charles could see (understand) things if he would, James would see things if he could.' Do you think this is a fair judgement of James?

The Glorious Revolution

William of Orange did not have to fight to win the **Glorious Revolution**. In fact, not fighting probably helped him to win. James II continued to lose support, while William did not risk creating sympathy for James by killing his followers. Even better, by making sure that James escaped as he was ready to enter London, William did not have to put James in prison. This might also have won James sympathy.

William stuck to what he had said in his **declaration** (see pages 58–9). Once in London, and in effect in control of the country, he called a Parliament. This is known as the **Convention Parliament**.

At first the House of Lords and the House of Commons disagreed about what should happen. Some wanted William to run the country but wanted to keep James II as King, though without any power. Others wanted to make William's wife, Mary, Queen. They believed that she would leave most of the government to William. William said that he would not act as a **regent**, or as his 'wife's gentleman usher'. Most people agreed that this was reasonable. This suggests that, 100 years after the defeat of the Spanish Armada, probably the greatest triumph of Elizabeth I's reign, many were not happy with having a woman ruler.

The House of Commons passed a very important **resolution** (Source A.) This was cleverly worded. The idea was to get support from as many people as possible.

- How did it appeal to people who hated Catholics?
- How did it appeal to people who were worried by any move to take away the power of the King? (These people were still worried by what had happened between 1640 and 1660.)
- How did it appeal to people who wanted Parliament to be more powerful?

Having agreed that the throne was vacant, Parliament decided who should sit on it. They offered the throne to William and Mary jointly, but only if William and Mary accepted their conditions. The conditions were known as the **Declaration of Rights**, later passed by Parliament and called the **Bill of Rights**. The Bill of Rights, together with some Acts of Parliament passed soon after, solved once and for all some of the questions that Parliaments and kings had argued about for most of the century:

Source A

'King James, having tried to subvert the constitution of the kingdom by breaking the contract between King and People, and by the advice of Jesuits and other wicked persons having violated (broken) the fundamental laws, and having withdrawn himself out of the kingdom, has abdicated the government and the throne is thereby vacant.'

Resolution of the House of Commons, Convention Parliament, 1689.

Source B

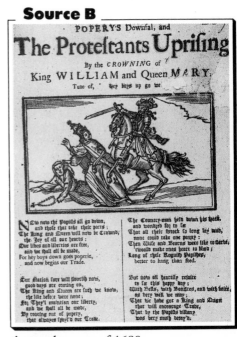

A popular song of 1689.

Religion The monarch could not be a Roman Catholic, nor could they marry one. Protestants who did not want to join the Church of England could have their own churches. However, the right to vote and the right to become an MP would be given only to people who were members of the Church of England.

Parliament Only Parliament could grant taxes and pass laws. There had to be a new Parliament **at least** once every three years.

The law The monarch could not suspend laws. Only Parliament could **repeal** (cancel) a law. Only Parliament could set up special courts to try unusual cases.

Money The cost of running the country was separated from the monarch's own finances. There was to be a special payment, the **Civil List**, to cover the monarch's personal expenses.

The army Control over the army was to be shared. The monarch would be the head of the army, but Parliament would have to pass an Act each year to give the monarch power to keep discipline in the army.

The Glorious Revolution of 1688–9 ended the conflict between King and Parliament that has dominated the first half of this book. Parliament was to be the more powerful of the two. Parliament had **chosen** the King and Queen, having **decided** that the throne was vacant. James I's idea of the **divine right of kings** was finished. Kings could be appointed by Parliament on the terms that Parliament thought fit.

This does not mean that government suddenly became fair. Most men did not have the right to vote, nor did any women. However, the idea of some democracy was safe. Between 1603 and 1689 many countries in Europe had gone through the same problems. In Europe it was usually the kings who won. In France, for instance, the **Estates General** (the equivalent of our Parliament) stopped meeting. The French King had the power to put people in prison without trial and the power to make whatever laws he wanted to. English men and women, by opposing things they thought were not just, had saved their liberty.

Questions

Section A

1 Write out these lists in their correct chronological order.

  a Declaration of Rights; William and his army reach London; William and Mary crowned; Convention Parliament first meet.

  b Monmouth's rebellion; James II crowned; Charles II crowned; death of Oliver Cromwell.

  c Execution of Charles I; the Glorious Revolution; the Eleven Years' Tyranny; the Pilgrim Fathers go to America.

  d The Great Fire of London; the Gunpowder Plot; Matthew Hopkins' persecution of witches; the Convention Parliament.

2 Who is being trampled in Source B?

Section B

Synthesis is the skill of bringing all the different parts of a story together and showing what the key points are.

3 Look back through this part of the book. Try to work out what James I, Charles I and Cromwell when he was Lord Protector would have felt about the conditions accepted by William and Mary. Ideas you could think about are religion, Parliament, law, money and the army.

4 Write definitions for these words: liberty; democracy; Parliament; law.

5 Do you think that what happened between 1603 and 1689 changed the way people looked at the ideas you wrote about in answer to question 4? Explain your answer.

Early Eighteenth-Century Britain

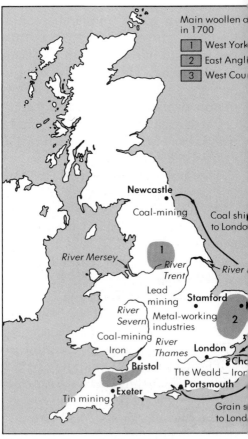

Britain in the early eighteenth century.

In 1700 the population of England and Wales was about six million people. Most of these people lived in small country villages growing just enough food in the open fields for their families to survive. In some areas people took on a second job making woollen cloth in their homes. This gave them a little extra income.

The most important person in the village was the squire, who lived in the manor house. He was the major landowner and had a lot of power over the ordinary villagers. The only really large city in 1700 was **London**, with a population of about 500,000 people. The West End of London was very fashionable, with fine houses and streets. Here lived the doctors, bankers, lawyers and merchants. These people met regularly in the **coffee houses** to smoke tobacco and discuss the politics of the day. In contrast, however, the East End was filthy and squalid. Here lived the poor, large numbers of them drinking their lives away in the many gin shops.

Bristol, with a population of 20,000, was a growing port, trading with Africa and America. In 1700 Britain already had control of a number of overseas **colonies**. These colonies provided raw materials and were also places where British goods could be sold. Trade was therefore very important to Britain, and this meant that a good navy was needed to protect the trade routes. Portsmouth and Chatham started to grow in importance as naval bases. Other important towns in 1700 were York, Norwich, Exeter, Stamford and Newcastle.

Some history textbooks have said that there was not very much industry in Britain in 1700. However, we are now realising that **industry** was showing signs of growth at this time, even though there were no large factories. Coal, for example, was mined in increasingly large amounts. London imported coal from Newcastle via ships that sailed down the coast. Lead was mined in Derbyshire and tin in Cornwall. Woollen textiles were made in East Anglia, West Yorkshire, Lancashire and the West Country. Metal industries were important in the West Midlands. Iron was made in the Weald area of Sussex and Kent and in South Wales, Shropshire and the Forest of Dean. The main method of transporting industrial goods was along major rivers or on ships around the coast of Britain.

Activity

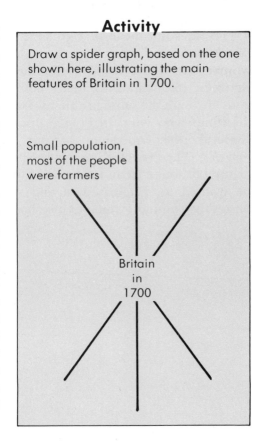

Draw a spider graph, based on the one shown here, illustrating the main features of Britain in 1700.

Small population, most of the people were farmers

Britain in 1700

Source A

*Every year in the village of Tichborne in Hampshire the squire
used to give presents of food to the poor. This was called the
Tichborne Dole. This painting of the occasion was done by Giles
von Tillborch in 1670.*

Questions

Section A

1 Find out the population of England and Wales today. How does it compare with the population in 1700?

2 Why was the squire a powerful person in the early eighteenth-century village?

3 Why was Bristol growing in importance?

4 'Industry was not very important in 1700.' Do you agree with this statement? Give reasons for your answer.

Section B

5 Study Source A. Draw up a chart like the one below to identify the people in the painting.

Person/people	How I identified them in the painting
Squire	
Upper-class people	
Servants	
Poor	

6 What evidence does Source A provide for historians about life in 1700?

7 Do you trust Source A as a piece of historical evidence? Give reasons for your answer.

Agricultural Revolution (1): Enclosures

In 1750 most farmland was cultivated under the **open field system**. Crops were grown on strips of land in huge fields which surrounded each village. Every landowner had strips scattered around all of the fields. But most villagers did not own any land, they were either tenant farmers who rented strips from the landowners or labourers who worked on other people's land. Each year wheat was grown in one of the great fields and barley or oats in another. A third field was always left **fallow** for a year to allow the soil to recover. Another area of land was always left uncultivated. This was the common land, where the villagers who had 'common rights' could graze their animals.

This open field system wasted land. The fallow field was the most obvious waste, but many of the landowners thought that the common land was wasted too. Time was also wasted. Farmers had to keep taking their tools, animals and seeds from one strip to another. The livestock also suffered. All of the animals mixed on the common land, so diseases spread and the best animals interbred with the worst. The open field system lasted for centuries, but then things changed. The population of Britain trebled between 1750 and 1850 from about 7 million to about 21 million. This meant more people needing food. The price of farm produce started to go up. There were big profits to be made by any farmers who could produce more, so some of them began to want to change the open field system.

Source B

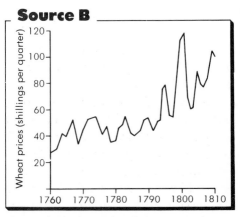

A graph showing the changes in wheat prices in the eighteenth century. Compare it with Source C.

Source C

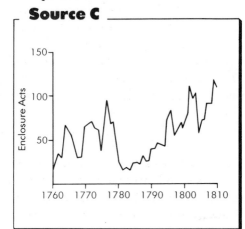

A graph showing the number of parliamentary acts of enclosure in the eighteenth century. Compare it with Source B.

Source A

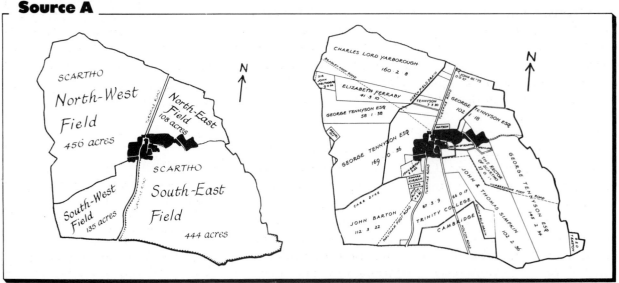

Scartho, in Humberside, before and after enclosure in 1795. Scartho had two great fields and two smaller fields, which made up the third area for crops. The common land is not shown on these maps.

Enclosures

In villages where there were only a small number of landowners, they sometimes got together and swapped strips so that each owner's land was brought together into a larger unit. Each owner could then **enclose** his land with hedges into several small fields and farm it separately. This was called **voluntary enclosure**. These farmers were seen to make more profits than the others.

Sometimes the landowners couldn't agree. In these cases, if the owners of 80 per cent of the land asked Parliament, they could get a law passed to force enclosure on the rest of the village. This was called **parliamentary enclosure**. In these cases, the law would usually include the common land in the land divided among the landowners. All those who lost common rights would get a share of land to compensate them.

Parliamentary enclosures became more and more common after 1750. There were 4,000 Acts passed between 1760 and 1810, enclosing over 5 million acres. These mainly affected the southern and midland counties.

The effects of enclosures

Enclosure Acts were expensive. Fees had to be paid to solicitors and surveyors, and then new hedges, paths and roads had to be built. The cost of all this was paid by the landowners. This was fine for the larger landowners, but some of the smaller landowners, called **yeomen farmers**, could not afford it and had to sell their land to pay their costs. Before enclosure, many landowners rented out most of their land in small units to tenant farmers. But after enclosure, most landowners wanted fewer tenants renting larger farms. Some tenant farmers had to take jobs as farm labourers. Farm labourers sometimes had cause for complaint too. The common land had been a valuable source of free firewood, fruit and berries, as well as a place to graze their chickens or pigs. Enclosure often divided up the common land among the landowners. Any tiny plot which labourers got as compensation was nothing compared with what they had lost.

The long-term effects of enclosures benefited most people, because they allowed farmers to adopt many new methods which were more efficient. The open field system had meant that all of the farmers had to agree about the way in which the great fields were cultivated. Because everyone shared the land, there was no room for variation. But with enclosed fields farmers could use their initiative to introduce any new methods they wanted to experiment with.

Source D

The costs of enclosure

	£	s	d
Legal charges	876	9	0
Parliamentary expenses	219	11	8
Commissioners' fees	1,284	9	4
Commissioners' expenses	251	7	10
Surveyor's fees	934	18	0
Roads and paths	1,030	11	4
Stakes and fences	184	1	1
Miscellaneous	916	2	3
Total	5,697	10	6

Common land in Sheffield was enclosed by an Act of Parliament in 1791. The costs involved in this enclosure are shown above.

Questions

Section A

1 Copy out the following paragraph, filling in the gaps using the words given below.

Many farmers were becoming fed up with the . . . . . by 1750. It wasted . . . . . and . . . . . . Food . . . . . were rising and there was a chance of bigger . . . . . for the most . . . . . farmers. Some . . . . . got together to agree to . . . . . their land, but others had to get . . . . . to force enclosure through.

landowners profits land
parliament open field system
prices enclose efficient
animals time

Section B

2 What did country people in the eighteenth century think about:
a the open field system?
b the common land?

3 Most Members of Parliament were landowners. Why do you think most requests for parliamentary enclosure were accepted by Parliament?

Agricultural Revolution (2): Other Changes

With enclosure, many new farming methods were tried. Some farmers, like **Viscount Townshend**, adopted the Norfolk four-course **rotation of crops**. This involved using one field for wheat, one for clover, one for barley or oats and one for turnips or swedes and swapping these crops around the fields every year. None of the fields had to be kept fallow, because the clover and the swedes naturally replaced the nutrients which the wheat, barley or oats used up. Better still, the fields of clover and swedes could be used to graze animals, whose manure would enrich the soil as they fattened on the crops. This rotation used all of the land and produced higher yields of grain and meat.

Other farmers experimented with new seeds or better ways of sowing. Traditionally, farmers sowed by walking up and down the fields, scattering or **broadcasting** seed on both sides of them as they walked. Much of the seed was wasted. **Jethro Tull** invented a **seed drill** which could be pulled along behind a horse, evenly planting the seed in rows and then covering them up as protection against the birds. Tull later invented a **horse-drawn hoe** which could be dragged through the fields, weeding between the rows of crops. Other arable farmers introduced light iron ploughs, threshing machines and drainage pipes.

Livestock was also improved by farmers who used their herds for **selective breeding**. This involved using selected animals to develop new breeds. **Robert Bakewell** developed the New Leicester sheep, and the Colling brothers bred the Durham shorthorn cattle. These animals could then be sold to rear herds of livestock which produced high yields of meat and wool or milk.

The importance of agricultural change

As a result of these improved methods, more and more food was produced. This was needed to feed the rapidly growing population. But it was also good for industry, because there was enough produced to keep food prices reasonably low. High food prices would have forced wages up, and this would have harmed many of the new businesses growing up in the Industrial Revolution. Farmers managed to feed the growing population with an ever smaller proportion of the labour force. This meant that there were plenty of spare workers from the land to work in the factories.

Questions

Section A

1 The diagram below represents the first year of a three-course rotation on open fields. Copy it into your book. Add diagrams for Year 2 and Year 3.

Year 1

Field A

Fallow

Field C   Wheat   Oats or Barley   Field B

2 The diagram below represents the first year of a four-year rotation on enclosed fields. Copy it into your book. Add diagrams to show Years 2, 3 and 4.

Year 1

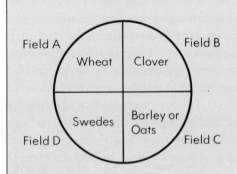

Field A   Field B

Wheat   Clover

Swedes   Barley or Oats

Field D   Field C

3 What were the benefits of:
   a the four-year rotation?
   b Tull's horse-drawn machinery?
   c selective breeding?

Section B

4 Study Sources A to E. Write a paragraph in support of, and a paragraph disagreeing with, the following statement:

'Bakewell was not the only farmer who experimented with selective breeding. He was not the most successful either. He doesn't deserve such a key place in the story of the agricultural revolution.'

Robert Bakewell – a case study

Robert Bakewell was a successful tenant farmer at Dishley Grange near Leicester. His New Leicester sheep were only briefly popular. They were soon overtaken by the Southdown sheep developed by Thomas Coke. But he remains one of the 'heroes' of the agricultural revolution, like Townshend and Tull. Textbook accounts always revolve around their work. But what was their role? What part did their actions really play in events? The sources and questions in this unit help you answer these questions.

Source A

'Bakewell replaced the old breeds of sheep which had been of use mainly for producing wool and manure with new breeds selectively reared for meat. They were heaviest in the best butcher's joints and came to their peak in two years and not four. Others followed. Within a century, the average weight of sheep at Smithfield Market rose from 28 lb to 80 lb.'

J. Steven Watson, 'The Reign of George III', 1960.

Source B

'In 1789, Bakewell's three best new Leicester rams were hired for 400 guineas (£420) each. Large hiring fees were helped by Bakewell's skill in publicity. He invited writers and painters to Dishley Grange where they were well wined and dined. They repaid him by describing his animals in magazines and painting them in oils. Each year he held viewings, rather like fashion parades, to show off the rams for hire.'

J. Robottom, 'A Social and Economic History of Industrial Britain', 1986.

Source C

A painting of a display of rams at Dishley Grange in 1809. Notice the prosperous-looking farmers in the background.

Source D

'Mr Toosey has for some years been a very attentive practiser of Bakewell's husbandry. His sheep are equally well made with the cattle; some few he sells for the breed, but for others he gets from 30s (£1.50) to £3 for two year olds from the butchers.'

Arthur Young, 'Tours in England and Wales', 1784.

Source E

Average weight of animals sold at Smithfield market in London

	1700	1800
Black cattle	166 kg	360 kg
Sheep	13 kg	36 kg
Calves	22 kg	66 kg
Lambs	8 kg	22 kg

The Domestic System

In the early eighteenth century the making of woollen cloth was the most important industry in Britain. Like many other industries, it was based on the domestic system, with the workers producing the cloth in their own homes. Women and children combed the raw wool; women spun it into thread; and men wove the threads into cloth on a loom.

Source A

'We saw the houses full of lusty fellows, some at the dye-vat, some at the loom, others dressing the cloths; the women and children carding or spinning; all employed, from the youngest to the oldest. Not a beggar to be seen, not an idle person.'

Daniel Defoe describing the West Yorkshire woollen industry in 1724. Defoe made his living from writing. He travelled the country writing down what he saw. However, one of his most famous books was a novel called 'Robinson Crusoe'.

Source B

'A job done by the children was the setting of wire teeth into cloth or leather for carding raw wool, a boring and often painful occupation, in which fingers must have got very sore and eyes very tired. Nevertheless, the children worked under the eyes of their parents, and were able to work without going away from home.'

Dorothy Thompson, 'The British People 1760–1902', 1969.

Source C

'They worked hard, sometimes exhaustingly hard, but at the same time they enjoyed a great deal of freedom. They were on their own without anyone to supervise them or give them orders. They could often work at their own speed and were paid for their work.'

L. W. Cowie, 'Industrial Evolution', 1975.

Source D

'There was no travelling to work. If they wanted they could take days off to follow the hounds or just idle and they lived in a healthy countryside. However, the workers' cottages were small, and they must have lived in an atmosphere of dusty wool. They were never sure when they would be paid.'

D. P. Titley, 'Machines, Money and Men', 1969.

Source E

'In those days many women were happy to spin. It was pleasant, light work. In the winter they did it by their cottage fires. In summer they would take their spinning wheels outside and gossip as they worked in the sunshine. Most of them were the wives of farm labourers and, as the men were badly paid, the families needed the money the women earned.'

P. F. Speed, 'History through Maps and Diagrams: The Industrial Revolution to Present-Day Britain', 1985.

Source F

Spinning and weaving in 1700.

Source G

The domestic system shown in a print from the time.

Source H

Spinning in the home, about 1700.

Questions

Section A

1 a How were the various jobs involved in making cloth divided up?
  b Why do you think this was done?

2 It is sometimes said that the domestic system was not well organised. Do you agree?

3 Copy and complete the chart below.

The domestic system from the worker's point of view	
Advantages	Disadvantages
1	1
2	2
3	3

Section B

4 a In what ways do Sources E and G agree?
  b Why do you think these two sources agree?
  c Does the fact the two sources agree mean they must be reliable?

5 a Which of Sources A,B,C,D and E is a primary source?
  b Is the primary source more reliable than the other sources? Give reasons for your answer.

6 Sources F, G, and H all give different impressions of the domestic system.
  a Which one do you think is the most accurate? Give reasons for your answer.
  b Which one gives the most glamorous picture of the domestic system?
  c Why do you think an artist might have wanted to give a glamorous picture of the domestic system?

7 Many history books say that child labour was first used in the factories of the Industrial Revolution. Is this true? Support your answer with reference to these sources.

Causes of Britain's Industrial Revolution

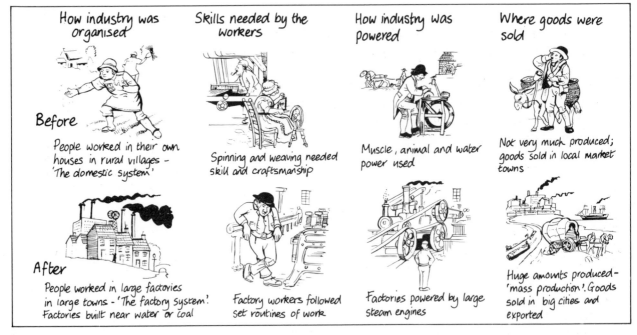

Changes brought about by the Industrial Revolution.

Between 1750 and 1850 Britain became an industrial country, with over 50 per cent of its population living in large cities and over 40 per cent of the labour force working in factories. In contrast, the numbers employed in farming steadily went downwards.

The changes shown in the diagram above are often called the **Industrial Revolution**. This, however, is only a label we use to make what happened easier to understand. Historians have said that the word 'revolution' is misleading, because it gives the impression of very rapid change. In fact, the changes were gradual and part of a process that had been going on for a long time. Another thing that historians have argued about is the reason why Britain became a country of factories, towns and industry. Some of the possible causes of the Industrial Revolution are listed below.

A

Britain had large amounts of **coal** to power the steam engines and plenty of **iron ore** to turn into iron.

B

Britain had lots of **individuals** who were prepared to risk their money in starting up new factories. Richard Arkwright and Matthew Boulton are just two examples.

C

Britain was a **peaceful** country. After 1750 no wars were fought in Britain.

D

In 1776 **Adam Smith** wrote a book called 'The Wealth of Nations' in which he said that the government should keep out of trade and industry. Smith said Britain would be better off if business people were left to get on without the government interfering. This policy, called *laissez-faire* (meaning 'leave alone'), was followed by the government.

E

There were a growing number of **banks** in Britain. This meant that people could borrow money to invest into industry.

F

Britain had **colonies** overseas. These provided British factories with **raw materials** (such as cotton). They were also **markets** for British factory-made goods.

G

British **agriculture** was becoming more efficient at this time, producing more food. People working in factories could therefore be fed.

H

Changes in **transport** – roads were improved and canals built – at this time meant that industrial goods could be moved about more easily.

I

There was a great interest in **science** and **technology**. Many **new inventions** were made (such as the steam engine) which helped to mechanise the factories.

J

The **population** of Britain grew rapidly between 1750 and 1850. This meant there was a much bigger demand for industrial goods. It also meant there were plenty of workers for the factories.

Questions

Section A

1 Make a list of the changes which took place in Britain between 1750 and 1850.

2 Is the term the **Industrial Revolution** a good one? Explain your answer.

Section B

3 Rank the causes of the Industrial Revolution into what you think is their order of importance. Explain why you chose this order.

4 Using the information in the boxes write a paragraph explaining why Britain had an industrial revolution.

5 Were all of these causes needed for the Industrial Revolution to happen?

6 One historian has written: 'It was the invention of machinery which meant the Industrial Revolution was bound to happen.' Do you agree? Give reasons for your answer.

7 Why do you think Britain was the first country in the world to have an industrial revolution?

The Textile Industry

The rapid increase in Britain's population after 1750 meant that there was a need for industry to produce goods in very large amounts. The domestic system could not meet such a demand. There was a need for factories and powered machinery. The first industry to change to such a way of working was the **Lancashire cotton textile industry**.

In 1733 John Kay of Bury invented a weaving machine called the **flying shuttle**. This was hand powered but it did speed up the weaving process. The hand-loom weavers of Lancashire were so angry that Kay had to run away to France. When Kay's machine came into widespread use after 1750, the hand-spinners were unable to keep up with the weavers, and there was a shortage of cotton thread. In 1764 James Hargreaves of Blackburn invented a new spinning machine called the **spinning jenny**. This could spin eight threads at one time – the spinning wheel produced only a single thread. Hargreaves's machine was small enough to be used in the home. It had the effect of balancing out the speed of spinning and weaving. By 1788 there were 20,000 spinning jennies in use. Like Kay, however, Hargreaves was not popular with the workers. His house was set on fire, and he fled to Nottingham.

In 1769 Richard Arkwright, a wig-maker from Preston, invented the **water frame**. This was another spinning machine, powered by water. It was too big for a house, so in 1771 Arkwright built a mill (or factory) at Cromford (Derbyshire) on the banks of the River Derwent. Arkwright was a very good business man and he went into partnership with Jedediah Strutt and Samuel Need. Between them they built more factories and made a great deal of money. Arkwright died in 1792, leaving £500,000.

The water frame, however, also caused some problems. First, it made spinning a much quicker process than weaving. Second, the thread it produced, though strong, was also very coarse. A machine was needed to spin thread that was both smooth and strong. In 1779, Samuel Crompton of Bolton invented such a machine. It was called the **mule**. It, too, had to be put into factories and it was powered at first by water and then by steam.

By now spinning was a much faster process than weaving. The hand-loom weavers had plenty of work and were happy with the situation. In 1784 the Reverend Edmund Cartwright, from Leicestershire, visited Matlock where he saw a lot of the new spinning machines in operation. He realised that the textile industry would be held back unless a weaving machine was invented that

Arkwright's mill at Cromford.

A spinning factory.

could work at the same pace as the spinning machines. In 1785 he invented a **power loom**. This was made of wood and was rather clumsy. Cartwright started up a factory in Doncaster but had difficulty in getting the machine to work properly. In 1803 William Horrocks of Stockport made an improved power loom out of iron. Further improvements were made by Richard Roberts. By the 1820s the machine was being used in factories and powered by steam. Gradually, the hand-loom weavers were put out of business.

The woollen industry was much slower to mechanise than cotton. Wool was a much older industry and had a lot of tradition and old rules. People in the woollen industry were against any changes. It was the West Yorkshire area which first built woollen factories. It took until 1850 for the woollen industry to become fully mechanised – about thirty years later than cotton.

Source D

'It was difficult to apply machinery to wool, the strands of which broke more easily than cotton. Another reason for the slow advance of machinery was the difficulty of increasing the supplies of raw wool, and it was not until wool was imported from Australia that the factory system could make much progress.'

R. Rundle, 'Britain's Economic and Social Development', 1973.

Source C

Cromford, Marh 2nd 1772

Sir,
Yours yisterday came to hand together with a bill from Mr Need. I am Determind for the feuter to Let no persons in to Look at the works. I am tired with riteing . . . and think you can scairsly Reed it. Excuse haist
And am yours' & Co,
R. Arkwright.

A letter written by Richard Arkwright to Jedediah Strutt.

Questions

Section A

1 Copy and complete the chart below:

	Inventor	Machine	Town
Kay			
Hargreaves			
Arkwright			
Crompton			

2 Use an atlas to find out which county each inventor's birthplace is in. What do you notice? How can this be explained?

3 Study Source C. Make a list of the spelling mistakes. Does it surprise you that Arkwright was bad at spelling? Give reasons for your answer.

4 Compare Source B with Source G on page 69. What differences and similarities can you see?

Section B

5 a Draw a diagram like the one below to show how the five main inventions led from one to another in a chain of cause and consequence.
  b Give the diagram a key and shade in *causes*, *consequences* and things which were *both*.

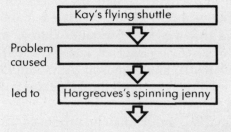

6 Arkwright is sometimes called **the father of the factory system**. Why do you think this is so?

7 Which of the five inventions described in this unit do you think was the most important? Give reasons for your answer.

Changes in the Iron Industry

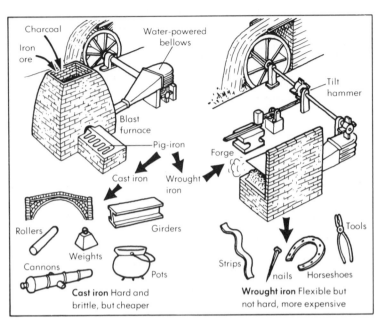

How iron was made in 1700.

In 1700 the iron industry faced a very serious problem: a shortage of timber to make charcoal for smelting iron ore. Timber was used for so many things, such as house-building and shipbuilding, that it was fast running out. If the iron industry was to expand, a new fuel for smelting had to be found. Some owners of iron-works, called **iron-masters**, tried to use coal, but without much success. Coal contains sulphur, which spoils the iron.

In 1709 Abraham Darby I became the owner of an ironworks at Coalbrookdale in Shropshire. Darby understood the problem and he started to experiment with using coal in his blast furnace. He found that if the coal was first turned into coke it could be successfully used for smelting. The coal near Coalbrookdale had a low sulphur content, and this was an advantage. Darby, who died in 1717, kept his discovery a secret, and it was left for his son (Abraham Darby II) and grandson (Abraham Darby III) to perfect the method. Not until the 1750s was coke smelting widely used.

Darby's method, unfortunately, produced only iron that was suitable for casting. A new method of making wrought iron was now needed. Wrought iron was the best quality iron. It was made in a forge by reheating and hammering (by hand) blocks of pig iron. It was slow and costly to make. Britain was forced to import wrought iron from Sweden and Russia.

Source A

'About 1709 he came into Shropshire to Coalbrookdale. He here cast iron goods in sand out of the blast furnace that blow'd with wood charcoal; for it was not yet thought of to blow with pit coal. Some time after he suggested the thought that it might be possible to smelt the iron from the ore in the blast furnace with pit coal; upon this he first try'd with raw coal as it came out of the mines, but it did not answer. He, not discouraged, had the coal coak'd into cynder and then it succeeded to his satisfaction. But he found that only one sort of pit coal would suit best for the purpose of making good iron.'

Abiah Darby, wife of Abraham Darby II, writing in 1775.

Source B

'The iron industry played a major role in British industrialisation. It provided cheaply the material on which modern industry was to depend for its essential equipment.'

Phyllis Deane, 'The First Industrial Revolution', 1965.

Source C

Year	Iron produced (tonnes)
1720	25,000
1788	70,000
1820	450,000
1850	2,000,000

Iron production 1720–1850.

Henry Cort is usually given the credit for discovering a new method of making wrought iron. He had an ironworks at Fontley in Hampshire and produced iron for the navy. Cort was unhappy with the fact that it took fifteen hours to make one tonne of wrought iron. In 1783 he devised a method called puddling. This involved using a reverberatory furnace (see diagram below). With this method it took one hour to produce fifteen tonnes of wrought iron. Also, the wrought iron could be taken straight from the furnace in a semi-molten (liquid) state and rolled into shape under large rollers. In this way pipes, girders and sheet iron could be quickly made.

The reverberatory furnace used for puddling.

Following these new improvements in iron-making, ironworks were built near to supplies of coal (see maps below and on page 82). Ironworks also became much bigger, with blast furnaces, foundries and forges all on the same site. Now that more iron was being produced, it was used for making many different things – machines, steam engines, iron rails, bridges, ships and locomotives.

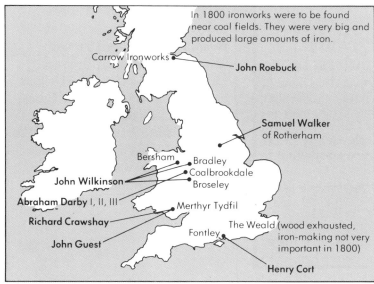

The iron industry in 1800.

Questions

Section A

1 Study the diagram 'How iron was made'. Write a paragraph describing how iron was made in 1700.

2 Why were blast furnaces sited near to forests in 1700?

Section B

3 Were the following causes of the discovery of new methods of making iron? In each case say 'yes' or 'no' and explain your answer.

 a A quickly growing population.
 b A shortage of timber.
 c Brilliant individuals.
 d Supplies of coal being available.
 e The growth of other industries, such as textiles and building steam engines.

4 Did Abraham Darby I make his discovery by accident? Explain your answer.

5 Darby made his discovery in 1709, but it took until the 1750s for it to be used widely. Why do you think there was this delay?

6 Some textbooks say that Peter Onions of Merthyr (in South Wales) discovered puddling and not Henry Cort. Does it matter who discovered puddling? Give reasons for your answer.

7 Which discovery was more important – smelting with coke or puddling? Give reasons for your answer.

8 What results did the new methods have for:

 a the iron industry?
 b other industries?

The Iron Bridge

In 1781 the world's first iron bridge was opened. Up to this time all bridges were made of stone, brick or timber. The new bridge spanned the River Severn near Coalbrookdale. Abraham Darby III and John Wilkinson have always been given the credit for the bridge. But why was the bridge built? Why was it built of iron? And were Darby and Wilkinson the only people involved? A study of some of the evidence may help us to answer these and other questions.

Source A

'The Severn Gorge had been a busy industrial area for many years. Many heavy cargoes had to be ferried across the river, and many people, too, had to cross the river to their work. The nearest bridges were at Buildwas and Bridgnorth, and the lack of a bridge in the Gorge itself must have been a severe handicap. There were several passenger ferries in the Gorge, but anyone who has seen the Severn in flood will realise how dangerous they would have been at certain times of the year.'

Barrie Trinder, 'The Iron Bridge', 1979. Barrie Trinder wrote this book after studying a wide range of primary and secondary sources. He is an expert on the history of the Iron Bridge.

Source B

> Clerk of the General Meetings.
> N. B. *Serjeants will attend from Twelve to Six in the Afternoon of the preceding Day, to provide those with Quarters who may come in on that Day.*
>
> ## A BRIDGE to be Built.
>
> ANY Person willing to undertake to Build a BRIDGE, of one Arch over the Severn, from Benthall Rail to the opposite Shore in Madeley Wood, in the County of Salop; of Stone, Brick, or Timber, the Arch One Hundred and Twenty Feet in the Span, the Superstructure Eighteen Feet Clear, the Centre of the Arch, Thirty Five Feet from Low Water; are desired to send Proposals to Thomas Addenbrooke, at Coalbrookdale, before the 20th of June next, and to Attend a Meeting of the Proprietors, at John Nicholson's, at Coalbrookdale, on Friday the 28th of the same Month, at Eleven o'Clock in the Forenoon.
> Coalbrookdale, 15th May, 1776.

Advertisement asking for people to build a bridge across the River Severn, 1776.

Source C

'In 1773 Thomas Farnolls Pritchard (1723–77), a Shrewsbury architect, wrote to John Wilkinson suggesting the building of an iron bridge in the Severn Gorge. Wilkinson loved new ideas, and it was entirely in character for him to be associated with a project like the Iron Bridge. Abraham Darby was appointed treasurer to the project. Pritchard was commissioned to prepare a design for the bridge, which Darby III agreed to build.'

Barrie Trinder, 'The Iron Bridge'.

Source D

'The people who provided money for the bridge included many of the leaders of local industry besides John Wilkinson and Abraham Darby III. Among them was Edward Blakeway (Wilkinson's partner), Edward Harries (lord of Benthall Manor), John Thursfield (surgeon and mineowner), John and Charles Guest (founders of the Dowlais Ironworks in South Wales) and Thomas Pritchard. An argument developed among the subscribers. Darby III and his supporters Pritchard, Wilkinson and Leonard Jennings wanted a bridge in iron. But a majority of the shareholders wanted a bridge of wood or stone.'

Barrie Trinder, 'The Iron Bridge'.

Source E

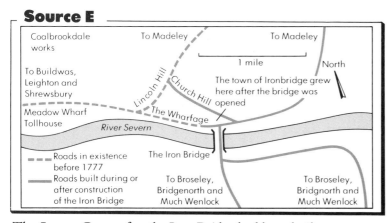

The Severn Gorge after the Iron Bridge had been built.

Source I

'Thomas Pritchard contributed substantially to the design of the bridge as it was finally built and was one of the original subscribers. The building of the bridge was undertaken by Abraham Darby III. He arranged for the payment of the workmen, and obtained building materials and tools.'

Barrie Trinder, 'The Iron Bridge'.

Source F

TABLE of TOLLS.

	s	d
For every time they pass over this **BRIDGE**.		
For every Coach,Landau,Hearse,Chaise,Chair,or such like }		
Carriages drawn by Six Horses,Mares,Geldings,or Mules. }		
Ditto ————— by Four Ditto ———	2.0	
Ditto ————— by Two Ditto ———	1.6	
Ditto ————— by One Ditto ———	1.0	
	0.6	
For every Horse,Mule, Ass,pair of Oxen,Drawing or Harness'd		
to draw any Waggon,Cart,or such like carriage, for each Horse&c	0.3	
For a Horse,Mule,or Ass, laden or unladen and not drawing,	0.4	
For a Horse,Mule, or Ass carrying double , —————	0.2	
For an Ox ,Cow, or neat cattle —————	0.1	
For a Calf, Pig, Sheep,or lamb —————	0.0	
For every Horse,Mule, Ass, or carriage going on the roads		
and not over the Bridge, half the said tolls.		
For every Foot passenger, going over the Bridge	0.0	

N.B. *This Bridge being private property, every Officer or Soldier, whether on duty or not, is liable to pay toll for passing over, as well as any baggage waggon, mail-coach or the Royal Family.*

The tolls charged for passing across the Iron Bridge.

Source G

'The bridge firmly stood, and dauntless braved the storm.'

'Salopian Journal', 18th February 1795, reporting flood waters on the Severn. Many houses on the banks of the river were swept away.

Source H

The bridge today.

Questions

Section A

1 Why, according to Source A, was a bridge across the Severn Gorge needed?

2 Why do you think a bridge had not been built earlier?

Section B

3 Copy out the following table. Then classify each source listed by putting a tick in the correct column.

	Source		
Primary	Secondary	Written	Artefact (object)
A			
B			
E			
F			
G			
H			

4 The Iron Bridge was opened in January 1781. Was it always certain that the bridge would be made of iron? Explain your answer.

5 Is it right that Darby and Wilkinson should have got all the credit for the Iron Bridge?

6 'The Iron Bridge was strong and also helped transport in the Severn Gorge.' Do you agree? Give evidence to support your answer.

7 Look back to question 3.
   a Which sources have you found the most useful in this unit?
   b Are primary sources more useful than secondary sources?

77

Early Forms of Power

In early eighteenth century industry the following forms of power were available: **human muscle power, animal power, wind power** and **water power**. All these methods had been used for centuries. Windmills were used for draining low-lying land and grinding corn into flour. Watermills were used for the same jobs and also powered textile machinery in the early factories and operated the bellows of blast furnaces in ironworks. They all, however, had problems. Once the factory system started to grow after 1750 it was clear that these traditional forms of power were not reliable enough. This led eventually to the steam engine being perfected by James Watt. Before this, factories were powered mainly by large waterwheels. Study the sources and find out about early forms of power.

Source C

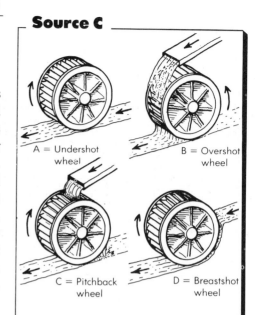

A = Undershot wheel
B = Overshot wheel
C = Pitchback wheel
D = Breastshot wheel

The undershot wheel was the oldest design. Large waterwheels in the eighteenth and nineteenth centuries were often the breastshot design.

Waterwheels.

Source A

An early eighteenth century horse gin.

Source B

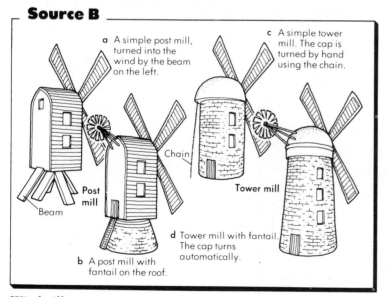

a A simple post mill, turned into the wind by the beam on the left.

c A simple tower mill. The cap is turned by hand using the chain.

Chain

Post mill

Tower mill

Beam

d Tower mill with fantail. The cap turns automatically.

b A post mill with fantail on the roof.

Windmills.

Source D

'29 May.   Another very warm day and this dry weather is much against us as the River Ribble is very low and in the afternoons our looms go very slow for want of water.

28 August.   There were 30 mills stopped in Blackburn this week for want of water, and will not start again until the wet weather sets in.'

A diary entry by a Lancashire weaver, late eighteenth century.

Source E

TO PERSONS CONCERNED IN
WATER WORKS.
TO BE SOLD,

At Ilkiston Cotton Mill, in the county of Derby;

A WATER WHEEL, close Buckets, suitable for either breast or overfall, 20 feet diameter, 6 wide; together with an excellent Shaft, and Spen Wheel, 16 feet diameter, with Cast Iron Segments; the whole in good condition, being nearly new.

Also, 6 Cast Iron Pipes, and 2 Working Barrels, 23 inches diamete, the Pipes 9, and the Working Barrels 10 feet long.

Ilkiston Cotton Mill is 9 miles from Derby, and 8 from Nottingham, close to the Erewash Canal, which joins the Cromford and Trent Navigations; the whole is now at work, and may be viewed at any time, and taken away after the 16th of March next.

Sale of a watermill, 1799.

Source F

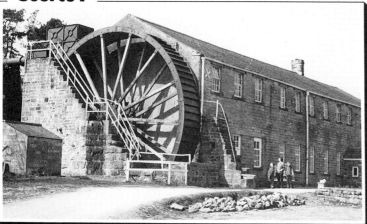

A large water wheel at Foster Beck Mill, Yorkshire.

Source G

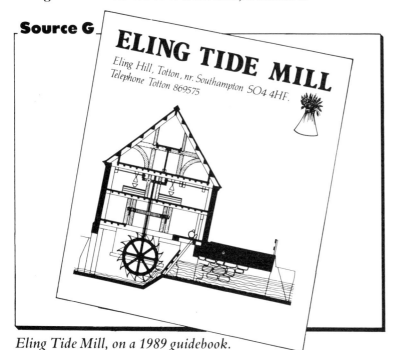

ELING TIDE MILL

Eling Hill, Totton, nr. Southampton SO4 4HF.
Telephone Totton 869575

Eling Tide Mill, on a 1989 guidebook.

Source H

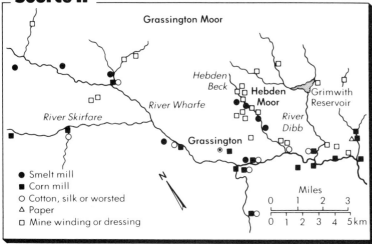

Grassington Moor

Hebden Beck

Hebden Moor

River Wharfe

Grimwith Reservoir

River Dibb

River Skirfare

Grassington

N

● Smelt mill
■ Corn mill
○ Cotton, silk or worsted
△ Paper
□ Mine winding or dressing

Miles
0   1   2   3
0 1 2 3 4 5km

Watermills in West Yorkshire, 1830.

Questions

Section A

1 Study Sources B, C and F. What changes in design can you see?

2 Why were these changes made?

3 Draw a spider graph to illustrate the defects of each early form of power. Use the sources to help you.

4 Why was there a need for a more reliable form of power after 1750?

Section B

5 'Once the steam engine was perfected in 1785, other forms of power quickly died out.' Does the evidence here support this statement?

6 Is Source E on its own of any use to the historian? Give reasons for your answer.

7 Is Source G a primary or a secondary source? Explain your answer.

8 'Buildings such as Source F cannot be biased, and therefore they are more useful to historians.' Do you agree? Give reasons for your answer.

9 People who study and photograph old industrial buildings and sites such as factories, railway stations and water mills are called 'industrial archaeologists'. How important is their work? Explain your answer.

James Watt and the Steam Engine

In 1698 Thomas Savery (1650–1715) built a steam engine to drain water from tin mines in Cornwall. He called it 'The Engine for Raising Water by Fire'. The engine was clumsy and dangerous but it pointed the way forward for other inventors.

In 1705 Thomas Newcomen (1663–1725), a blacksmith from Dartmouth, started to build a steam engine which would also be used to drain mines. In 1712 the first Newcomen engine was put into use at Dudley Colliery in the West Midlands. This engine (see Source A) was a big improvement on Savery's and was used in many coal mines. There were over 100 at work in the Northumberland and Durham coalfield by 1775. However, Newcomen's engine could be used only for pumping water and it was also very expensive to run because it used so much coal. If the steam engine was to be more widely used, it needed to be much cheaper to run.

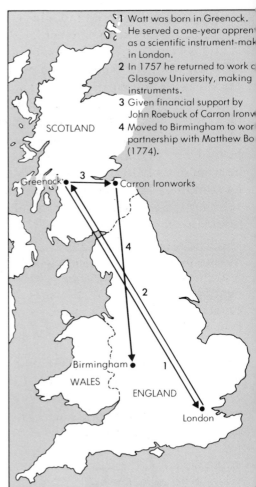

1 Watt was born in Greenock. He served a one-year appren— as a scientific instrument-mak— in London.
2 In 1757 he returned to work c— Glasgow University, making instruments.
3 Given financial support by John Roebuck of Carron Ironw—
4 Moved to Birmingham to wor— partnership with Matthew Bo— (1774).

A map of summarising the life of James Watt (1736–1819).

Source A

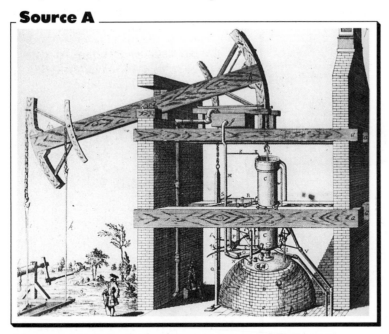

Newcomen's engine had only one use – pumping water.

In 1763, just by chance, James Watt was asked to repair a model of a Newcomen engine. Watt worked in Glasgow, making instruments for the University there. He soon saw the design faults in this engine and began to puzzle about how they could be overcome. How could he make an engine which used less coal? In the end he invented a separate condenser (see diagram). This meant less fuel was needed. Now he needed someone to give him financial

Source B

'From 1775 onwards James Watt and Matthew Boulton, in a classical partnership of inventor and businessman, were producing new-type steam engines. In 1782 Watt went on to patent rotary motion. From this time onwards it was possible to use the steam engine as the means of motive power in factories. Necessity was certainly the mother of this invention.'

Asa Briggs, 'The Age of Improvement', 1959.

backing so that he could build his engine. This person was Dr John Roebuck, the owner of the Carron Ironworks. With his help Watt built a steam engine to his new design. In 1773, Roebuck went bankrupt. It seemed as if Watt's career as an inventor was over until Matthew Boulton (1728–1809) came to the rescue. Boulton was the owner of the Soho Works, a large hardware factory in Birmingham. He saw that Watt's engine had a great deal of promise and he told Watt he was prepared to provide him with money if he went to work in Birmingham. Watt probably felt that he had nothing to lose and in 1774 moved south.

In 1781 Watt, helped by William Murdoch (Boulton's foreman and a brilliant engineer), devised a rotary motion steam engine which used sun-and-planet gears. Boulton borrowed £17,000 from the bank to put this new machine into production. His gamble paid off. By 1800 there were over 500 Boulton and Watt engines at work in a wide range of factories. Watt was also helped by John Wilkinson, the iron-master, who invented a lathe which could produce accurately bored cylinders. With rotary motion the steam engine could be used to drive machinery in textile mills, flour mills, breweries and iron foundries, as well as in canal-building. Watt's engine needed accurately made parts in order to work efficiently, and this led to the growth of precision engineering.

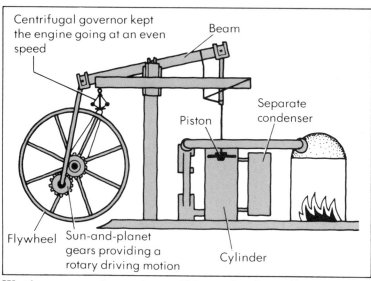

Watt's rotary motion engine could be used to drive all sorts of machines.

Source C

'Glasgow, a town with a university, had a reputation for scientific research. Watt's advance owed much to his university connections.'

Christopher Harvie, 'The Industrial Revolution', 1972.

Source D

'Boulton's craftsmen had trouble boring the long accurate cylinders that Watt needed. Boulton put the work out to John Wilkinson. Wilkinson sent a trial cast-iron cylinder to Watt in April 1775. It was so well made that even Watt could not find fault with it, and he was a perfectionist. Boulton and Watt were in business.'

John Wilkes, 'United Kingdom', 1984.

Section A

1 Draw a time-line showing the main events in Watt's life.

2 What does Asa Briggs mean by a 'classical partnership'?

3 Draw a spider graph to show the results of the rotary motion steam engine.

Section B

4 Both Savery's and Newcomen's engines had big faults. Does this mean that these two men were not important? Explain your answer.

5 The fact that Watt worked in Glasgow was of great importance. Do you agree?

6 Pick out two key events in the life of James Watt. Explain why they were key events.

7 'Watt could have succeeded without Murdoch and Wilkinson but not without Boulton.' Do you agree? Give reasons for your answer.

8 'The rotary motion steam engine was the most important invention of the Industrial Revolution, and James Watt was the most important person.' Do you agree? Give reasons for your answer.

Coal Mining: Problems

In the early eighteenth century coal was mined in a number of ways (see diagram 1).

These methods were ideal when the coal was near to the surface. But by 1750 most of the surface coal was used up – just at the time when the demand for coal was increasing. People needed coal to burn on their fires; wood was running out and had become very expensive. Many industries were using coal as a fuel, including the iron industry, brick-making, brewing and soap-boiling. All of these industries were themselves growing quickly. The increased use of the steam engine also required more coal.

Britain was lucky. In many areas of the country (see map) deep beneath the ground, there were vast amounts of coal. When landowners such as the Duke of Bridgewater, Earl Fitzwilliam and the Duke of Sutherland discovered coal beneath their estates they were willing to risk money to mine it. Money was needed because the only way the coal could be reached was by digging **vertical shafts**. As the years went by, mines became deeper and deeper. By the 1830s many mines were 300 metres deep.

Deep shaft mining caused a lot of problems. The mines were liable to flooding, especially after heavy rain. Usually, an endless chain of buckets operated by a horse gin was used to drain the mines. This was not a very effective method. Getting coal to the surface was also a problem. Windlasses and hemp rope were used in many mines, but in Scotland women carried coal to the surface by climbing a series of ladders. Lighting was also a problem. There was no electricity, and miners often worked by the light of luminous fish-skins or candles. These methods were far from satisfactory.

Deep beneath the earth's surface there are lots of dangerous gases. Choke-damp is one; it is made up of carbon dioxide and could cause suffocation and choking. To overcome this, two shafts were sunk into the ground. At the bottom of one was a furnace. The idea was that the warm foul air would rise out of the mine. Another dangerous gas was fire-damp or methane. This lurked in the coal seams and would explode if it came into contact with a naked flame. In many collieries firemen were employed to deal with this hazard. Wrapped in wet sacking, they descended the mine before the day began. They crawled along with a long pole with a candle on the end trying to ignite small pockets of methane.

Not until about 1850 were solutions found to these problems connected with **shaft mining** (see pages 84–5).

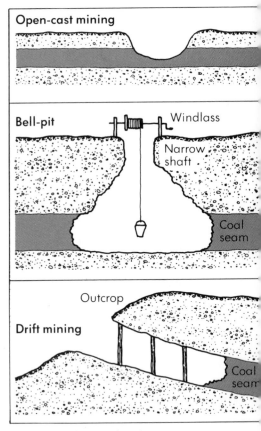

1: Early forms of coal mining.

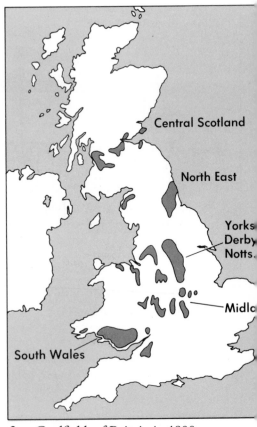

2: Coalfields of Britain in 1800.

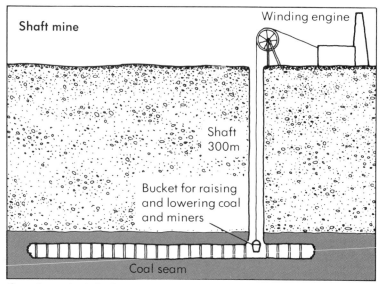

Shaft mine

Winding engine

Shaft 300m

Bucket for raising and lowering coal and miners

Coal seam

3: A vertical shaft mine.

Questions

Section A

1 Construct a flow diagram using the outline below. Put the heading *'The causes of mining problems in the late eighteenth century'*.

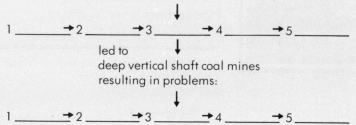

Increased demand for coal caused by:

1 _____ → 2 _____ → 3 _____ → 4 _____ → 5 _____

led to
deep vertical shaft coal mines
resulting in problems:

1 _____ → 2 _____ → 3 _____ → 4 _____ → 5 _____

Section B

2 The diagram above shows a causal chain. What does this mean?

3 If the population had not increased, would there still have been problems in mining coal in the late eighteenth century? Explain your answer.

4 Why do you think landowners were willing to dig coal mines on their estates?

5 Were the problems of deep shaft mining connected in any way? Explain your answer.

6 Why do you think it took until 1850 to solve the problems of shaft mining?

7 It has been said that 'The stories of coal, iron and steam are linked together.' Do you agree? Give reasons for your answer.

Early attempts to deal with explosive gases.

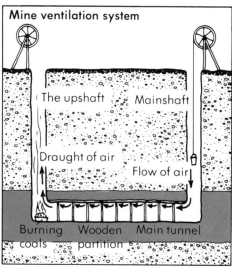

Mine ventilation system

The upshaft   Mainshaft

Draught of air

Flow of air

Burning   Wooden   Main tunnel
coals   partition

4: Early attempts to ventilate mines.

Coal Mining: New Methods

In the late eighteenth and early nineteenth centuries new methods and techniques were introduced into coal mines to overcome the problems described on pages 82–3.

Source A

A colliery in the eighteenth century.

Source B

A Staffordshire colliery in the nineteenth century.

Source C

'Watt's rotative engine was ideal for hauling coal to the surface. Steam haulage was not, however, in general use until the introduction of wire cables in the 1840s.'

R. J. Cootes, 'Britain Since 1700', 1968.

Source D

'Flooding was largely overcome with the introduction of the steam engine. During the eighteenth century Newcomen's and later Watt's engines were widely used in coal mines all over Britain.'

D. P. Titley, 'Machines, Money and Men', 1969.

Source E

'In 1807 John Buddle, the manager at Wallsend Colliery, devised his exhaust fan, which was an air pump to provide the ventilation necessary to get rid of choke-damp.'

C. P. Hill, 'British Economic & Social History, 1900–75', 1977.

Source F

'Twenty-six children were drowned in Moorside pit on the afternoon of 4 July 1838. A violent thunderstorm broke over the village, and water began to run down the hill to the mine up which forty boys and girls were coming. As they passed through a ventilating door a rush of water was heard coming towards them. Fourteen managed to get into a cavity in the wall, but the rest were trapped by the water, and drowned.'

John Addy, describing a flood in a mine in South Yorkshire, in 'A Coal & Iron Community in the Industrial Revolution', 1969.

Source G

Moving coal to the shaft. From the Report of the 1840 Royal Commission.

Source H

'Many of the changes were introduced only towards the middle of the nineteenth century, and many districts remained notably backward. While the new forms of ventilation were in general use, along with steam pumps, in the North of England by 1850, they were slow to be adopted in other coalfields, such as Shropshire, South Staffordshire, Warwickshire, South Wales and Scotland.'

Neil Buxton, 'The Economic Development of the British Coal Industry' 1978.

Source I

'The flame was enclosed in a wire gauze, and as it would not pass through this gauze, outside gases could not be ignited. One result of the invention was to encourage coal-owners to work more difficult and dangerous seams.'

J. Thurkettle describing the miners' safety lamp in, 'An Outline of the Social and Economic History of Britain 1066–1956', 1968.

Questions

Section A

1 What new methods were introduced in the early nineteenth century to cope with the following problems in the mines?

　a Flooding.
　b Getting coal to the surface.
　c Choke-damp.
　d Lighting.
　e Fire-damp.
　f Moving coal from the coal face to the shaft.

2 a What differences in mining methods can you see between Source A and Source B?
　b What similarities in mining methods can you see in Source A and Source B?
　c Do you think the new methods were used in every coal mine in Britain?

Section B

3 You have been asked to produce a chapter on 'New Methods of Mining' for a book. You have been given a maximum of 500 words for this task. Write your chapter, selecting your sources from this unit.

4 Compare your chapter with those of three other people.

　a How far are the chapters different?
　b If they are different, does this matter?
　c Did you find the task easy or difficult? Explain your answer.

The Miner's Safety Lamp

Who invented the safety lamp?

In 1812 there was a terrible explosion at Felling Colliery, Gateshead. Ninety miners were killed. The Reverend John Hodgson was so appalled that he formed the Sunderland Society for the Prevention of Accidents in Mines. In August 1815 Hodgson asked **Sir Humphrey Davy** if he could make a lamp which could be used in a mine without igniting fire-damp. Davy visited the North-East to investigate, returned to London to work on the problem and, within three months, had invented the **safety lamp**. This is the most commonly told story of how the miner's safety lamp was invented. However, **George Stephenson** claimed to have invented the safety lamp before Davy and there was a huge row which went on for many years. Who was the first to invent the safety-lamp?

George Stephenson (1781–1848)
Stephenson was born in Wylam, Northumberland. He came from a working-class family. He found writing and spelling very difficult but he was excellent at engineering. He is famous for inventing steam locomotives and building railways such as the Liverpool to Manchester.

Sir Humphrey Davy (1788–1829)
Davy came from Cornwall and was the son of a Methodist preacher. He became a brilliant scientist and chemist. He was a lecturer at the Royal Institution and was very famous by 1815.

Source A

Stephenson with his lamp, 4 June 1881.

Source B

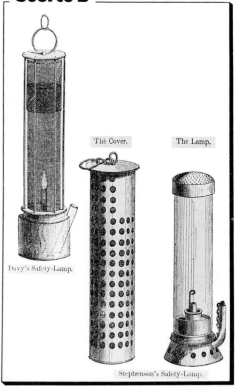

The safety lamps of Davy and Stephenson.

Source C

'Beyond reasonable doubt, the important initial breakthroughs in idea and design were made by Davy.'

Neil Buxton, 'The Economic Development of the British Coal Industry', 1978.

Source D

'On 21 October 1815, Stephenson's first design for a safety lamp was tested at Killingworth Colliery. Davy produced his design for a safety lamp on 9 November 1815. Davy's invention was undoubtedly an original effort, and his reputation as a scientist secured for it considerable publicity.'

W. O. Skeat, 'George Stephenson: The Engineer and His Letters', Institute of Engineers, 1973.

Source E

'From letters which have turned up, we know that Davy had been working behind the scenes to discredit Stephenson, using Hodgson as a front man. In a letter dated 8 February 1816, Davy wrote: "Stevenson is not a man whose word is worth anything. He is a thief."'

Hunter Davies, 'George Stephenson: A Biographical Study', 1975. Hunter Davies comes from the North of England.

Source F

'Killingworth, 13 March 1817

Sir,

I stated to several persons, long before Sir Humphrey Davy came into this part of the Country, the plan of such a lamp was seen by several, and the lamp itself was in the hands of the manufacturers during the Time he was here.'

Stephenson replying to the 'Philosophical Magazine', which had accused him of stealing Davy's ideas.

Source G

'The latest lamps made by Mr Stephenson are imitations of the lamps of Sir H. Davy'.

Tyne and Wear Coalowners, November 1817.

Source H

'There was an enormous amount of evidence to show that Stephenson had done practical tests from August 1815'.

Hunter Davies.

Source I

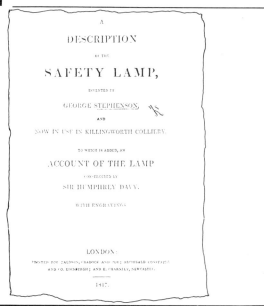

A DESCRIPTION OF THE SAFETY LAMP, INVENTED BY GEORGE STEPHENSON, AND NOW IN USE IN KILLINGWORTH COLLIERY. TO WHICH IS ADDED, AN ACCOUNT OF THE LAMP CONSTRUCTED BY SIR HUMPHREY DAVY. WITH ENGRAVINGS

LONDON: PRINTED FOR BALDWIN, CRADOCK AND JOY; ARCHIBALD CONSTABLE AND CO. EDINBURGH; AND E. CHARNLEY, NEWCASTLE. 1817.

Title page of Stephenson's book describing his safety lamp.

Questions

1 a Why do you think Source A was drawn?
   b Is this source reliable?

2 Does Source A prove that Stephenson was the first to invent the safety lamp?

3 Study Source B. How similar are the two lamps?

4 Are Sources E and H biased? Give reasons for your answer.

5 Study Sources D and F. Davy visited the North-East on 24th August 1815. In Source F Stephenson says that his lamp was actually being made when Davy first visited. Could Stephenson have been telling lies? Give your reasons.

6 What was Davy's opinion of Stephenson?

7 Why do you think Stephenson included Davy's lamp in his book? (Source I.)

8 Which of the following do you think is the most likely explanation? Give reasons for your answer.

   a Davy stole Stephenson's ideas
   b Stephenson stole Davy's ideas
   c Both men invented a safety lamp while working on their own.

9 Why do you think Davy has always been given more credit for the safety lamp than Stephenson?

10 Does it matter who invented the safety lamp first? Give reasons for your answer.

Wedgwood and the Pottery Industry

A portrait of Wedgwood.

In 1700 pottery was a localised domestic industry. Often farmers made and sold pottery to increase their income. By 1800 pottery had become a major factory-based industry centred on the North Staffordshire town of **Stoke-on-Trent**. Why did this change come about?

- By 1750 the **population** of Britain had started to grow very quickly and there was a much bigger demand for pottery.
- Social habits were changing with **tea-drinking** growing in popularity.

The main reason why it was North Staffordshire which supplied this increased demand was the ability of **Josiah Wedgwood** (1730–90). Wedgwood was born in Burslem into a family of potters. While in his teens he caught smallpox, which resulted in the amputation of his left leg. This disability, however, did not stop Wedgwood from going into the pottery trade. He was so successful that by 1766 he was able to build a large factory near Stoke called Etruria. Here Wedgwood made a large range of top-quality pottery.

In 1769 Wedgwood went into partnership with Thomas Bentley. Together they thought up a number of ideas for selling pottery:

- They advertised their pottery in magazines.
- They had catalogues printed.
- They opened a display shop, run by Bentley, in London.
- They offered refunds to anyone who had a complaint about the quality of the pottery.

Etruria Hall, 1770.

A view of the Etruria works showing the canal.

Activity

Working in groups of six organise a paper aeroplane factory. You have an order for twenty planes. You have the following materials: A4 paper, scissors, rulers and felt-tips. The planes should have a company logo marked on and should be made using A5 size paper.

- Three people should make the planes using division of labour.
- Three people should make the planes as individuals.

Discover which group of three people gets the best results.

Source D

The Etruria Works.

Wedgwood built up a long list of regular customers and began to export goods to Europe. Perhaps his most famous customer was Catherine the Great of Russia, who commissioned him to make a 952-piece dinner service.

In his factory, Wedgwood used a method called **division of labour**. Each worker had his or her own specialised job to do in the production process. Some prepared the clay; some shaped the soft clay; and some fired the pottery in the large 'bottle ovens'. This method was much more efficient than one person trying to carry out all the processes on their own. Wedgwood demanded high standards – if his sharp eye detected second-rate work he would smash the pot and chalk on the worker's bench: 'This will not do for Josiah Wedgwood.' The rules in the Etruria factory were very strict. But in return, the workers were given housing, and schools were provided for their children.

In 1782 Wedgwood was one of the first factory owners to buy one of Boulton and Watt's new rotary motion steam engines (see pages 80–1). This was used to crush flints which were used in the preparation of the clay.

One serious problem which faced Wedgwood was that of **transport**. The roads in and around Stoke were narrow and bumpy. So pottery was often smashed on its way to market. Wedgwood was quick to see the advantages that a **canal** would bring. In 1766 he became one of the main supporters of a plan to build a waterway linking the River Trent with the River Mersey. The canal, called the **Grand Trunk Canal** (and now called the Trent and Mersey Canal – see page 95), was started by James Brindley and finished in 1777. Much of the money was provided by Wedgwood.

Questions

Section A

1 Study Sources A and B. Do these sources on their own tell us anything about Wedgwood? Explain your answer.

2 Study Source C. Name the canal in the picture. Why is it built so near to the factory?

3 'Etruria was more than a factory. It was a community.' Do you agree? Support your answer with evidence.

4 Using the map on page 95, explain why Wedgwood was so keen on canals.

Section B

5 It is often said that Wedgwood had foresight – the ability to plan for the future. Give two possible examples of this and explain each one.

6 'Wedgwood had great determination and high standards.' Do you agree? Support your answer with evidence.

7 Both Watt (Unit 2.10) and Wedgwood had partners. Both were successful. Why do partnerships often succeed?

8 Was Wedgwood born at the right time and in the right place? Give reasons for your answer.

Road Improvements and Turnpike Trusts

In 1555 an Act was passed saying that each **parish** had to look after its own roads. The men of each parish had to work for six days in the year on repairing the roads, without pay. Often the local unemployed men were put to work on the roads in return for dole money from the parish poor fund. Also one man had to serve as the **surveyor**. It was his job to organise the labourers and to get local farmers to provide wheelbarrows, spades and stones. If he failed to do this he could be fined by the local magistrates. The parishes with the hardest job were those which happened to lie on busy routes like the Great North Road. Many roads were in a terrible condition – swamps in winter and full of hard ruts in the summer. Travelling was usually slow and often dangerous.

In the late eighteenth century there was an urgent need for roads to be improved. Factories were starting to develop and they needed to get goods to market. They also needed to bring in raw materials such as cotton and coal. With the growing population there were more people living in towns. Farmers needed good roads so that they could transport food into the towns. Also firms needed to send out mail advertising their products.

Source A

Road menders in Yorkshire early nineteenth century.

Source B

'The road from Witney to North Leach is, I think, the worst turnpike I ever travelled in; so bad that it is a scandal to the country.'

Arthur Young, 'A Six Weeks Tour through the Southern Counties', 1769.

Source C

'Turnpikes were not supervised by any central authority, so the standards of roads varied. Many people claimed that most of the money was used to line the officials' pockets instead of paying for better roads.'

Colin McNab and Robert Mackenzie, 'From Waterloo to the Great Exhibition', 1982.

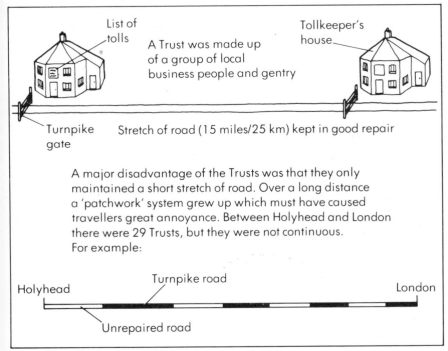

List of tolls

A Trust was made up of a group of local business people and gentry

Tollkeeper's house

Turnpike gate

Stretch of road (15 miles/25 km) kept in good repair

A major disadvantage of the Trusts was that they only maintained a short stretch of road. Over a long distance a 'patchwork' system grew up which must have caused travellers great annoyance. Between Holyhead and London there were 29 Trusts, but they were not continuous. For example:

Turnpike road

Holyhead

London

Unrepaired road

How a Turnpike Trust operated.

The government did very little to improve the road conditions. At that time people in the government did not agree with getting involved in local affairs (this was part of the belief called **laissez-faire**). Instead, the roads were improved by local business people, farmers and traders. They formed **Turnpike Trusts**. Each Trust got permission from Parliament to take over a stretch of local road. They erected barriers at each end of the road and charged travellers a **toll** to use the road. The tolls were meant to go towards the cost of keeping the road in good repair.

Turnpike roads were not always welcome, and in some areas the tollgates were smashed down. During the eighteenth and early nineteenth centuries, however, the number of Turnpike Trusts increased: from 380 in 1748, to 530 in 1770, to 1,100 in 1830. In 1830 Turnpike Trusts had control of 22,000 miles (35,200 km) of road out of a total of 105,000 miles (168,000 km) in the whole of Britain.

Questions

Section A

1 a During which period were most Turnpike Trusts set up across the country as a whole:
   1748–70 or
   1770–1830?
  b Why was this?

2 a During which period were most Turnpike Trusts set up in Nottinghamshire:
   1725–65 or
   1765–1830?
  b Does Nottinghamshire fit in with the national trend? Support your answer with evidence from the sources.

3 'The turnpike system grew up in an unplanned way.' Do you agree with this statement?

Section B

4 What would people in each parish have felt about having to keep the local roads in good repair? Explain your answer.

5 The improvement of the roads would have helped Britain's industry. Why, then, didn't the government do more to help?

6 a Who do you think would have been in favour of a turnpike road in the local area and why?
  b Who do you think might have been against a turnpike road in the local area and why?

Source D

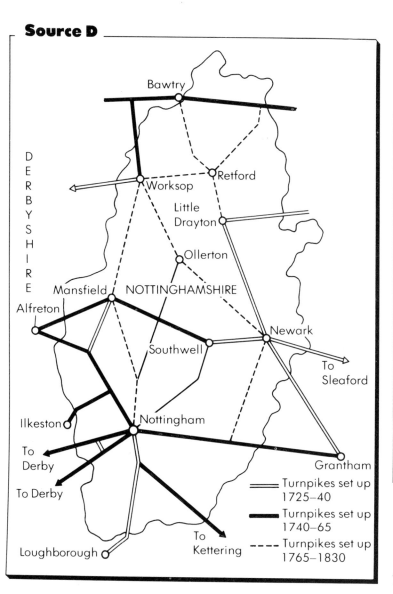

Turnpike roads in Nottinghamshire.

91

Road-Building Methods

During the period 1760–1830 road-building methods improved greatly. Three men were responsible for this. **John Metcalfe** (1717–1810) built 180 miles (288 km) of good road in Yorkshire, Lancashire and Cheshire. **Thomas Telford** (1757–1834) built 900 miles (1,440 km) of road. He improved the road from Shrewsbury to Holyhead. One of Telford's greatest achievements was the Menai Straits suspension bridge, opened in 1826, which linked this road from mainland Wales to the island of Anglesey. **John McAdam's** (1756–1836) method of road building was simple but effective. McAdam became the consultant engineer to many Turnpike Trusts and wrote a successful book called *The Present State of Road-Making*.

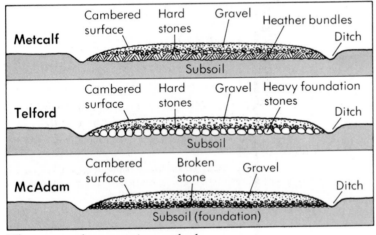

The new road construction methods.

The improved roads resulted in a boom in **stage-coach travel**. Stage-coach companies competed for customers on the main routes, keeping to a scheduled timetable. Companies made claims as to which had the fastest and most reliable service. **Coaching Inns** also enjoyed good business. They would provide food and rest for the passengers and fresh horses for the coach. By 1837 there were over 30,000 people employed in the stage-coach trade – as drivers, coach-makers, stable-lads and innkeepers. Many historians refer to the years 1815–40 as the 'golden age of coaching'. The **Royal Mail** was also now carried in special Mail Coaches, an idea first thought of by John Palmer of Bath in 1784. Before this, post-boys on horseback had delivered the mail. The better roads also meant that goods could be transported more quickly.

Questions

Section A

1 Study the diagram showing the new road construction methods. Why do you think most Turnpike Trusts used McAdam's method?

2 Make out a chart like the one below and classify Sources A to F.

Primary	Secondary	Reason
A		
B		
C		
D		
E		
F		

Section B

3 Does Source A tell you anything about Telford? Explain your answer.

4 a Why do you think Source B was produced?
  b Is it reliable?

5 a People had to pay to get an entry in a trade directory. Why would they be prepared to do this?
  b What evidence can be obtained from a Directory?
  c What are the main problems historians will have when using a trade directory?

6 a Is Source C a cartoon? Give reasons for your answer.
  b How useful is Source C to the historian?

7 Source F is from a novel. Novels are fiction. Does this mean that it is useless to the historian?

8 What do you think was the aim of the author of Source E?

9 Do you think the phrase 'the golden age of coaching' is a good one for the period 1815–40? Give reasons for your answer.

Source A

The Menai Straits Bridge.

Source B

STAGE COACH PASSENGERS AT BREAKFAST

Inside a coaching inn in the early nineteenth century.

Source C

The White Horse Inn, London, drawn in 1835.

Source D

BISHOP's WALTHAM.

ALLINGTON, Mrs. Milliner
Apſe, William, Wheelwright
Apſe, John, ditto
Arnold, Edward, Brewer
Baker, Thomas, *the Dolphin Inn*
Baynes, James, Tanner
Baynes, Robert, Brewer
Budd, William, Glazier
Bullock, John, Watchmaker
Churcher, John, Upholſterer
Cleve, Richard, Tanner
Cleve, William, Collar-maker
Colpas, Thomas, Carpenter
Colpas, Charles, ditto
Cole, Richard, Schoolmaſter
Cole, William, ditto
Colebourne, Robert, *the King's Head Inn*
Compton, James, Taylor
Cook, Thomas, *the White Hart Inn* (Poſt Chaiſe)
Donneger, Elizabeth, Poſt-Miſtreſs
Earwacker, Thomas, Staymaker
Fox, Thomas, Merchant
Godwin, Richard, Surgeon
G 3

Gunner, William, Attorney
Hayter, John, Shoemaker
Hayter, William, Butcher
Hewitt, Chriſtmas, Carpenter
Hogſdale, John, Collar-maker
Honeyman, Thomas, Grocer
Houghton, William, Butcher
Houghton, John, Baker
Hounſom, William, Blackſmith
Jennings, William, Bookſeller, Stationer, and Schoolmaſter
Jonas, Daniel, Miller
Jonas, Thomas, Maltſter
Jones, Jemima, Schoolmiſtreſs
Lacey, William, Attorney
Leach, Thomas, Barber
Lee, George, Brewer
Marett, Charles, Attorney
Martin, Elizabeth, Ironmonger
Mears, Richard, Tanner
Naſh, William, Grocer
Newlyn, William, Shoemaker
Offgood, Robert, Currier
Patbury, Thomas, *the Old King's Head*
Patbury, William, Blackſmith
Parjunt, William, Miller
Penford, James, Surgeon
Pignall, , Barber
Prior, Thomas, Grocer
Richardſon, Solomon, Blackſmith
Rockley, John, *the Queen's Head*
Sparſhot, Peter, Soapboiler

Veck,

'Sadler's Trade Directory' for Bishop's Waltham a small market town in Hampshire, 1784.

Source E

'As for those cosy inn scenes, meal stops were brief. Only 25 minutes were allowed to swallow a dinner costing 5s or 6s (25p or 30p) – and even that was reduced if the coach was late.'

Kevin Heneghan 'Travel by Uneasy Stages' writing in the 'Daily Telegraph', 1985.

Source F

'The weather was bitterly cold; a great deal of snow fell from time to time, and the wind was intolerably keen. They were little more than a stage out of Grantham, when Nicholas was suddenly aroused by a violent jerk. He found that the coach had sunk greatly on one side, though it was still dragged forward by the horses. The vehicle then turned easily over, flinging him on to the road.

A stage-coach journey described in Charles Dickens's novel, 'Nicholas Nickleby', 1839.

The Canal Network

Canals are inland waterways built by people. Inland waterways, in the form of rivers, had been used as a way of moving goods for centuries. Often, however, rivers are not **navigable** (suitable for large boats) because they are too shallow and have many twisting bends or rapids. The main rivers used for transporting goods in the early eighteenth century were the Thames, Dee, Trent, Severn and Humber. After 1750, as the population started to increase and factories began to develop, there was a need to move large amounts of industrial goods. Rivers could not be depended on (they often did not flow where they were needed), and roads were only just beginning to improve.

Between 1759 and 1761 the first British canal was dug linking Worsley with Manchester, a distance of 10 miles (16 km). The canal was the idea of the **Duke of Bridgewater**, who owned a colliery at Worsley. Pack-horses were being used to carry the coal into Manchester. This was costly, and the price of the coal was so high that few people could afford it. John Gilbert, the Duke's agent, employed James Brindley to build the canal.

Brindley took the canal over the River Irwell by building a magnificent aqueduct at Barton (See Source A, page 96). The canal was a big success. It cut the cost of transporting the coal. The Duke made a large profit by charging tolls to let local factory owners use the canal.

Brindley went on to even bigger things. He believed that the canal network should link inland areas with the ports of Liverpool, Bristol, Hull and London. Birmingham would be the inland centre of this network, which would form the shape of a 'X'. No one else – not even the government – planned the canal network. But Thomas Telford, John Rennie, James Barnes and William Jessop helped to complete the system.

The 1790s were known as the 'Canal Mania'. During this time Parliament gave permission for over fifty canals to be built. Some of them were not very successful. This was especially true of those canals built in the South of England such as the Basingstoke Canal (opened in 1794). The canals in the North of England were built to carry heavy industrial goods (such as iron, coal, timber, stone and bricks) and generally made good profits. They had been built for a definite purpose rather than just as part of the canal craze.

In 1830 Britain had 4,000 miles (6,400 km) of canals. But by the 1840s the network had started to decline. By this time the much faster and more efficient **railways** had

Source A

'Legging' on the Grand Union Canal.

Activity

Today our roads are overcrowded, with huge lorries transporting industrial goods. Canals now carry very little industrial traffic; most of our canals are used for pleasure cruising. Some people have suggested modernising the canals to carry more goods. This would ease pressure on the roads.

Organise a class debate on this issue. Form six groups to represent each of the following interests:

- Road hauliers
- The Department of Transport
- Holiday firms that hire out canal boats
- British Rail
- Conservationists and ornithologists
- Anglers

Each group should prepare its arguments, issue leaflets explaining its case and make up slogans. You will need to use libraries and search out information. A group spokesperson should present your case in the debate. (Props and costume would make the debate more lifelike.) After this, a free vote should take place on the issue.

Thomas Telford	**James Brindley**
1793 Started to build Elesmere Canal	1759 Started the Worsley Canal
1801 Started to build Caledonian Canal	1762 Made a survey for the Cheshire Canal
1805 Pont Cysyllte aqueduct finished	1765 Made engineer for the Calder Navigation
1822 Caledonian Canal finished	1766 Started Grand Trunk Canal
	1767–72 Made surveys for eight canals including the Leeds–Liverpool Canal.

caught on. Canal boats towed by horses were very slow in comparison with the railways. Canal boats averaged only about 3 miles (5 km) per hour! Also, the many different canal companies had built their canals to different widths. Some were built to take boats which were 20 feet (6 metres) wide, while others could take only narrow boats 13 feet (4 metres) wide. This lack of standardisation made through-traffic between different canals impossible. Railway companies often bought out the canals.

Questions

1 Draw a time-line which illustrates the growth of the canal network. Use the text and the map to help you.

2 Were each of the following causes of the canal mania? In each case say 'yes' or 'no' and explain why.

   a the increase in population
   b brilliant engineers
   c the growth of factories
   d the success of the Worsley Canal
   e the poor roads and lack of navigable rivers
   f the government

3 Study Source A.

   a What was 'legging'?
   b When do you think this photograph was taken?

4 Who do you think made the greatest contribution to the canal network: Brindley, Telford or the Duke of Bridgewater? Give reasons for your answer.

5 Why did most of the canals in the South of England fail and most in the North succeed?

The complete canal and river network.

Building a Canal

Building a canal was a very big and costly operation. In most cases the following things happened:

Stage 1 An **advertisement** was put in the local newspaper, telling people that a meeting was going to be held to discuss the building of a canal between two places.

Stage 2 At the meeting a **committee** was formed to plan the canal. An engineer was appointed to survey a route for the canal and to work out how much it would cost to build. At this stage people were asked to make promises of money for the scheme.

Stage 3 Now an **Act of Parliament** had to be passed, giving the canal promoters the right to buy land and raise money. A Bill was drafted, saying why the canal was needed and how much it would cost. This was debated in the House of Commons and then studied by a committee of the House. The committee called witnesses and asked them questions about the proposed canal. At this stage anyone who was against the canal could make their objection. But they had to go to London to do this. When the committee was satisfied that the proposed canal was a good idea, the Bill was passed by Parliament and became an Act. Lawyers would now be paid.

Stage 4 The **canal company** now issued **shares** to raise money. People could buy shares for about £100 each. (When the canal was opened, shareholders would each receive a share of any profits made.)

Stage 5 **Land** was bought up over which the canal was to pass. Some landholders were stubborn about selling and they held on for the best price they could.

Source B

'At Barton, James Brindley has erected a navigable canal in the air; for it is as high as the tops of trees.'

The 'Annual Register', 1763.

Source C

'As well as businesspeople and landowners, almost every social group in the country bought shares except the poor. Professional people found money; so did clergymen, widows, and Oxford dons.'

P. F. Speed, 'The Growth of the British Economy 1700–1850', 1980.

Source D

'The smiths' forges, the carpenters' and masons' workshops were covered workshops, which floated on the canal and followed from place to place.'

John Philips describing Brindley's working method, 'A General History of Inland Navigation', 1793.

Source A

Brindley's aqueduct at Barton carrying the Worsley Canal over the river Irwell, 1761.

Source E

'Sometimes the opposition was overwhelmed; sometimes it was persuaded by lining of the pocket or by giving shares. Special compensation was paid when the line of the canal cut house from farm, or farm from road. The Grand Junction paid £5,000 to Lord Clarendon for the right to pass through Grove Park.'

Charles Hadfield, 'British Canals: An Illustrated History', 1984.

Questions

Section A

1 a Draw a flow diagram showing the stages in building a canal.
  b At what stage did the canal company start buying up land? Explain why this was so.
  c How does Source A show the ways the problems of building canals were overcome?

2 At one stage James Brindley was the engineer for six canals at the same time. What does this suggest about the way he worked?

Section B

3 Study Sources A and B. Many people went especially to see the Barton Aqueduct. Why do you think they did so?

4 Buying shares can be a risk. Why do you think so many people were willing to buy canal shares?

5 Poor people could not afford to buy shares. Would poor people therefore have disapproved of canals? Give reasons for your answer.

6 What did landowners and farmers feel about canal-building?

Stage 6 The engineer could now start building the canal. Usually a contractor was called in to organise the work and provide the navvies (labourers). If the canal needed a lot of locks, tunnels or aqueducts, it would take a long time to complete. Wharves, warehouses, lock-keepers' houses and offices would also have to be built along the canal. Some canals took ten years to build.

Stage 7 At last the canal would be opened for trading. Money was raised by charging boats tolls for using the canal. If the canal was not used much, no profits were made, which left the shareholders very unhappy!

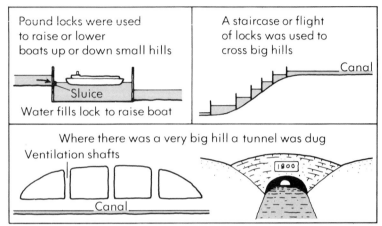

Engineering a canal.

Source F

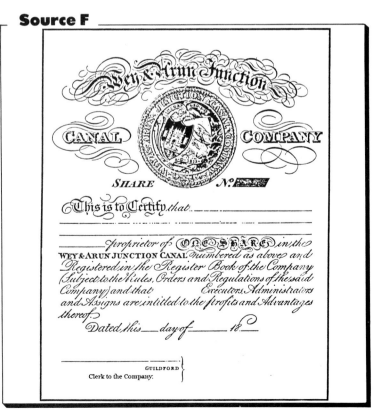

A share certificate for the Wey and Arun Canal, 1813.

97

The Growth of the Railways

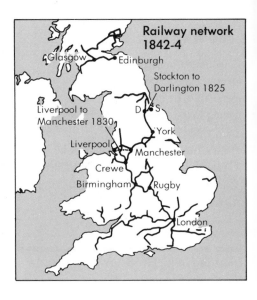

The period from 1844 to 1847 is often called 'Railway Mania'. It was a period of fast growth for the railways on a scale unknown before. Why did this boom take place?

Wooden railway tracks had been used in coal mines since the seventeenth century. Then, in 1767, Abraham Darby II successfully made rails out of cast iron. In 1781 James Watt invented the rotative steam engine for driving machines in factories. It seemed only a matter of time before a high-pressured steam engine was mounted on to wheels to make a locomotive. However, this did not happen until 1804, when Richard Trevithick built a locomotive called *Catch-Me-Who-Can*. His work was followed up by other men, including William Hedley, John Blenkinsop and George Stephenson. Many people still thought horse-drawn railways were the best idea.

In 1825 the **Stockton to Darlington Railway** was opened to carry coal. It was built by **George Stephenson** and at the opening his locomotive, *Locomotion No. 1*, was used. But people were still suspicious of the locomotive. In 1830 the **Liverpool to Manchester Railway** was opened, again the work of Stephenson. The directors were not sure what form of power to use on the line – horses, stationary steam engines operating belts or locomotives. In 1829 they held the Rainhill Trials to test the efficiency and safety of the locomotive. Stephenson's Rocket won the competition with an average speed of 15 miles per hour (25 kph).

The Liverpool to Manchester Railway was a big success. Other railways soon followed. In 1838 the first inter-city line between **London and Birmingham** was built by Robert Stephenson. Then, in 1841, the **Great Western Railway**, built by **Isambard Kingdom Brunel** was opened. This line linked London with Bristol.

In the early 1840s there was a trade depression. People were worried about putting money into railways. If the factories were not selling goods, there would be less need for railways and profits would drop. As a result, people did not rush to buy shares in railway companies. This all changed in 1844, when trade suddenly improved. Factories started to do well; employment was high; people were buying goods; and there was plenty of money about. With new confidence the public rushed to buy railway shares. Between 1844 and 1847 Parliament gave permission for 9,375 miles (15,000 kilometres) of railway to be built. By 1850, over 6,000 miles (9,600 kilometres) of railway line had been built.

Source A

'The Liverpool and Manchester Railway was successful from the start. In the three years 1831–3 the railway carried a daily average of 1,100 people. Receipts from the carriage of goods were also good. Taking the proceeds of both classes of traffic together, the profits were enough to enable the company to pay its shareholders an average dividend of 9.5 per cent every year from 1831 to 1845'.

Jack Simmons, 'The Making of the British Railways', 1968.

Source B

'It was no ordinary time. The pulse of the people, fierce and excited, grew by what it fed on. As every new project unfolded its prospectus, it demanded a greater stimulus and more extended action. From week to week, and from month to month, the madness continued to spread.'

J. R. Francis, 'History of the English Railway', 1851.

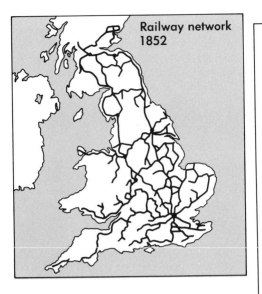

Railway network 1852

Source E

RAILWAY UNDERTAKING.

Touter. " Going by this Train, Sir?" *Passenger.* " 'M? Eh? Yes."
Touter. " Allow me, then, to give you one of my Cards. Sir."

A cartoon of the time.

Source C

'Why did the railways come? The answer, of course, is: because of the Industrial Revolution. The new factories, the new towns, the larger population, the increased volume of goods which had to be carried created the need for a faster means of transport. The Railway Age began on 15 September 1830, the day on which the first modern railway, the Liverpool and Manchester, was opened with steam locomotives from the first.'

Harold Perkin, 'The Age of Railways', 1970.

Source D

'Railways were a much quicker, cheaper and safer way to carry goods than roads or canal. Cuts in transport costs meant goods were much cheaper to buy. Industrialists could bring raw materials to their factories and send finished goods to their markets more cheaply. Cheaper goods increased demand.'

L. Hartley and Jon Nichol, 'The Industrial Revolution', 1985.

Questions

Section A

1 Draw a time-line showing the development of railways, 1767–1847.

2 a What was Railway Mania?
   b How do the maps show the effects of Railway Mania?
   c Did the author of Source B approve of Railway Mania? Give reasons for your answer.

3 a Did the artist of Source E approve of railways? Give reasons for your answer.
   b Are cartoons such as this of any use to the historian?

Section B

4 How far back in history is it necessary to go to explain the causes of the Railway Mania of 1844–7? Give reasons for your answer.

5 What event would you say 'triggered off' the Railway Mania of 1844–7? Give reasons for your answer.

6 Source C suggests that the Industrial Revolution as a whole was a cause of the growth of railways. Were the Railways also a cause of the Industrial Revolution? Give reasons for your answer.

7 Do you think Railway Mania would have happened if the Liverpool to Manchester Railway had been a failure? Explain your answer.

8 Which was more important in the growth of the railways – events or people? Give reasons for your answer.

Building the Railways

Building a railway line was a huge undertaking. As far as possible the track had to be kept level, because a steep slope would cause the wheels of the locomotive to slip. For this reason, **tunnels, cuttings,** and **embankments** had to be made to keep the track level. The diagrams below illustrate some of the problems and how they were overcome.

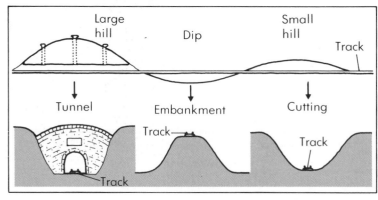

Some problems in building a railway line.

The 'navvies'

Railway building needed a large work-force with a variety of skills. The **navvies** or labourers were a class apart. It was their job to do the digging and earth-shifting. They cut out rock, dug-out cuttings and blasted out tunnels. This was hard, physical and dangerous work. Some of the toughest navvies could move 20 tonnes of soil in a day. Some of the navvies came from Ireland, some were from the English Fenlands and some were descended from the 'navigators' who had built the canal network between 1760 and 1830.

By the 1840s these men had developed a culture of their own. They travelled from line to line and lived in temporary huts or shanty towns. A number of them had 'larger than life' reputations. Stories about heroic feats and fights were part of their folklore. Many of them had nicknames usually derived from the town they came from (such as 'Contrary York' and 'Concertina Cockney'). As well as working hard the navvies played hard. At the weekends they would descend on the nearest town in search of a good time in the local alehouses. Many of them gambled and played wild games such as 'follow the leader' racing over the top of a tunnel leaping over the ventilation shafts as they went. Bare-knuckle fighting was also a favourite pastime. Without the navvies, however, the railway network – so vital to the process of industrialisation – would never have been built.

Activities

Much of the work of the navvies is still part of the landscape. Study the map below taken from an Ordnance Survey (OS) map. (Sheet 185).

1 Draw a similar diagram using your own area and describe the main features on the line.

2 Is there any evidence on your map of disused railways? If so, give details and try to explain the possible reasons for this.

Section of the railway between London and Southampton, originally built by Thomas Brassey in 1839.

Source A

Building the Kilsby Tunnel on the London to Birmingham Railway in 1838.

Source B

Employment on the Railways

Year	Navvies working	Miles of track in use	Railway employees
1847	250,000	3,000	45,000
1850	60,000	6,300	60,000
1855	40,000	8,100	100,000
1860	55,000	10,200	125,000

Source C

'The building of the Woodhead Tunnel on the Manchester to Sheffield Railway claimed many casualties among the navvies. Henry Pomfret, a surgeon, reported "32 dead, 23 cases of compound fractures, 74 simple fractures and 140 cases of serious burns from the blasting and lacerations."'

Terry Coleman, 'The Railway Navvies', 1968.

Source D

'One workman would build a hut for his family and also lodge some of his fellow navvies. Some huts contained as many as fourteen or fifteen men. Many were filthy dens.'

Terry Coleman, 'The Railway Navvies', 1968.

Source E

'The Midland Railway Company encouraged the civilising influence of the Bible and helped with the appointment of scripture readers. James Tiplady, a preacher, arrived at Batty Green, a shanty town of between 300 and 400 navvies and their ladies and over 100 children. There was no church so he preached in the open air.'

W. R. Mitchell and David Joy, 'The Settle to Carlisle Railway', 1973.

Source F

'Bread was baked in nearby Settle and brought up to Batty Green. Beef-on-the-hoof was driven there and slaughtered to feed the navvies.'

Terry Coleman, 'The Railway Navvies'.

Source G

A railway navvy, 1855.

Questions

Section A

1 Study Source B. Why do you think the number of navvies decreases, yet the number of railway employees increases?

2 Study Sources A and C. Why was the building of a tunnel dangerous work?

3 Study Source G. What does it tell you about the navvy's way of living?

Section B

4 If a navvy's job was so tough, why did so many men take up the work?

5 What would have been the attitude of the local people when the navvies were in their district?

6 Why do you think the Midland Railway Company (Source E) was prepared to employ a preacher? Give reasons for your answer.

101

The Impact of Railways

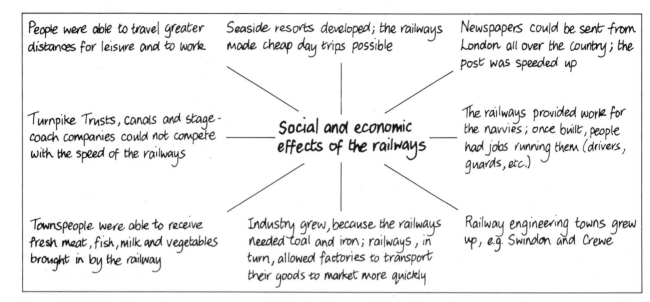

People were able to travel greater distances for leisure and to work

Seaside resorts developed; the railways made cheap day trips possible

Newspapers could be sent from London all over the country; the post was speeded up

Turnpike Trusts, canals and stage-coach companies could not compete with the speed of the railways

Social and economic effects of the railways

The railways provided work for the navvies; once built, people had jobs running them (drivers, guards, etc.)

Townspeople were able to receive fresh meat, fish, milk and vegetables brought in by the railway

Industry grew, because the railways needed coal and iron; railways, in turn, allowed factories to transport their goods to market more quickly

Railway engineering towns grew up, e.g. Swindon and Crewe

There is a range of different source material giving us evidence about the effects that the railways had on the country. This unit will enable you to interpret the sources and draw some conclusions about the effects of the railway on one community, Itchen Abbas in Hampshire. When historians use sources like this, they often find that the sources do not tell them everything they wish to know. So historians cannot always draw **definite** conclusions.

The social and economic effects of railways.

Section of the Tithe Map of Itchen Abbas, 1839

Source A

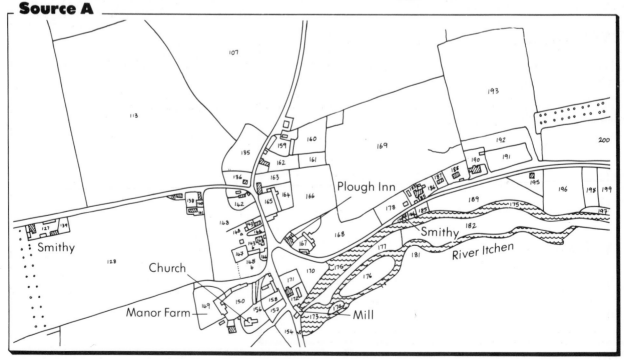

Source B

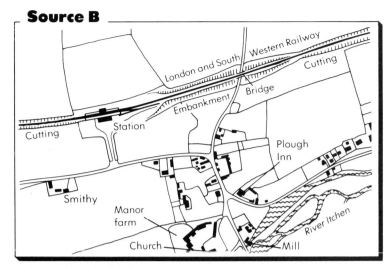

Itchen Abbas in 1870.

Source C

...ll Sarah, schoolmistress Miss ‖ Munday Miss S. ...ell James, carpenter and ...t., Plough ...ell James, jun. wheel- ...ight and beerhouse ...er James, blacksmith ...win Thos. blacksmith ...Enos, baker and shopr.	Sawkins Wm. corn miller Sheffard Thos. parish clerk Spicer Rev. Wm. Webb, M.A. *Rectory* White Wm. shoemaker and shopkeeper Wright Mrs. Eliza FARMERS. French Saml., *Moody's Farm*	Dear Henry ‖ Hayes Thomas Rogers Wm., *Rogers' Farm* Munday Miss Sarah POST OFFICE at Job Stan- brook's. Letters *via* Win- chester CARRIERS pass daily to Al- resford, Winchester, &c.

Extract from Kelly's Directory 1857.

Source D

COMMERCIAL.	POST OFFICE.—James Drover, receiver. Letters arrive from Alresford at 9 a.m.; dispatched at 6.15 p.m. The nearest money order office is at Alresford
...ell Peter, wheelwright ...dy Jane (Mrs.), baker ...er & Son, blacksmiths ...th William, *Plough* ...edge Henry, farmer	Here is a Board school: a school has been erected with residence for the mistress; Nathaniel Bailey, in 1837, left £10 per annum to be applied to school purposes at the sole discretion of the rector; Miss Costin, mistress
	Railway Station, Henry Hooper, station master

Aubert Major William, The Lodge
Corrie John Malcolm, The Elms
Gillson Rev. Septimus M.A. Rectory
Grey Stafford
Howard Capt. Hon. Cecil Ralph, Itchen cottage
Wynne Mrs. Garden cottage

Vokes William, miller, corn & manure merchant, Itchen Abbas mill
Way George, farmer, Manor farm
White Henry, painter
White Mary (Mrs.), shopkeeper
Wiltshire James, farm bailiff to Lord Ashburton, Itchen down

Extract from Kelly's Directory 1880.

Source E

Itchin Abbas – Birth places of residents		
Birth place	1861 (Before railway)	1881 (After railway)
Born in Itchen Abbas	92	68
Born elsewhere in Hampshire	92	105
Born outside Hampshire	30	71
Total population	214	244
Source: Census returns for 1861 and 1881		

Census Figures for 1861 and 1881.

Questions

Section A

1 How would the following have benefited from the railway?

  a the local farmers
  b the local miller
  c the publican
  d ordinary villagers

Section B

2 Study Sources A and B.

  a What changes in the look of the village can you find between 1839 and 1870?
  b If these were the only sources available, what could historians say about the year the railway was opened?

3 Study Source B. What engineering problems faced the builders of the railway?

4 Study Sources C and D. What changes took place in the facilities and services available in the village?

5 Study Source E.

  a Turn each figure into a percentage.
  b Draw two bar-charts for each year.
  c What differences can you see?
  d Was the railway responsible for these differences? Explain your answer.

6 Which of the sources in this unit do you think is:

  a the most useful?
  b the least useful?

Explain your answer.

The Great Exhibition

By 1851 Britain was the world's leading industrial country – the 'workshop of the world'. British factories supplied the world with goods, and British firms provided banking and insurance services for much of the rest of the world. London was the most important city in the world.

Prince Albert, the husband of **Queen Victoria**, had the idea of staging a huge exhibition in London where every country in the world would be invited to display the products of their industry. Albert said that such an exhibition would encourage friendship between different countries. But many people were against the idea, including many MPs and *The Times* newspaper. A site was bought in Hyde Park. Architects were invited to design a building for the 'Great Exhibition of the Works of Industry of All Nations'. The design accepted by the organising committee was that of Joseph Paxton, the head gardener of the Duke of Devonshire. It consisted of a building made entirely of glass and steel. When built, it was 1,867 feet (569 metres) long and 410 feet (125 metres) wide. *Punch* magazine called the building the **Crystal Palace**.

The Great Exhibition cost well over £300,000 to put on. It was opened by Queen Victoria on 1 May 1851 among great celebrations. There were almost 14,000 exhibits on show, over half of them British.

Source B

'It is probable that no other people in the world could have achieved such a marvel of constructive skill as the Crystal Palace. It is to our wonderful industrial discipline that we owe all the triumph.'

The 'Morning Chronicle', 1851.

Source C

'This is one of the greatest and most glorious days of our lives, with which, to my pride and joy, the name of my dearly beloved Albert is associated for ever. The Green Park and Hyde Park were one mass of densely crowded human beings, in the highest good humour and most enthusiastic. I felt much moved.'

Queen Victoria writing in her Great Exhibition Journal, 1 May 1851.

Source A

Source D

'England, as you are aware, reserved half of the Crystal Palace for the exhibition of its own products. While the foreign part of the exhibition is filled with objects of art, the English is principally occupied with objects of utility.'

A French visitor to the Exhibition.

The Crystal Palace in Hyde Park.

Source E

'It is the greatest imposition ever to be palmed upon the people of this country. The object is to introduce among us foreign stuff of every description. The dearest wish of my heart is that the confounded building might be dashed to pieces.'

Colonel Sibthorp MP, 1851.

Between May and October the Exhibition attracted over six million visitors; many of them were ordinary workers and labourers. From Mondays to Thursdays there was specially reduced admission price of one shilling (5p). The highest attendance for a single day was 109,915.

The Exhibition made a profit of £186,000. This was used to build the Royal Albert Hall, the Science Museum, the Natural History Museum and the Victoria and Albert Museum. All of these places are now visited by millions of people every year.

Questions

Section A

1 Why was the Crystal Palace an unusual building?

2 What point is being made in Source F about British industry in 1851?

3 'People today are still feeling the benefits of the Great Exhibition.' Can this statement be true? Give reasons for your answer.

Section B

4 Why was Queen Victoria so excited about the Great Exhibition?

5 What was the attitude of the British towards foreign countries and foreign people in 1851?

6 Many ordinary working people visited the Great Exhibition.

   a Why was this possible in 1851?
   b How would these people have felt about visiting London?

7 The Great Exhibition was a big success. Why, then, were many people against it happening? Give reasons for your answer.

Source F

SPECIMENS FROM MR. PUNCH'S INDUSTRIAL EXHIBITION OF 1850.

'Punch' cartoon showing a different view of the Great Exhibition.

Source G

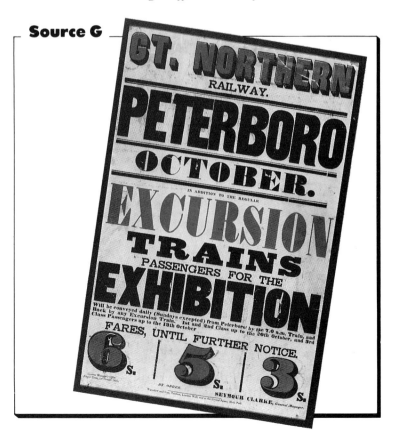

Railway poster for the Great Exhibition.

Working Conditions in Factories and Mines

When people began to build factories towards the end of the eighteenth century, there were very few regulations about working conditions. Some employers took advantage of this. There were complaints about low wages and long hours, as there always had been. There was also concern about child labour, although children had always helped their parents in workshops and the fields. The major new concerns were the **dangers to health** in the factories and mines; noise, heat and overcrowding; and the **exploitation** of women and children. Women were usually paid half and children a third of a man's wage, so many employers were tempted to employ them to do work more suited to full-grown men. Another complaint was the **loss of independence**. The factory bell and the relentless machines ruled the lives of workers used to controlling their own hours and methods of work.

Source A

'In this trade, [fork grinding], 855 perish out of every 1000 between 20 and 40 years of age, while in England and Wales the average is only 296.'

The 'Medical Times', 1843.

Source B

Fork grinders in Sheffield, 1866. Notice that despite the spray of sparks and metal dust, few workers are wearing goggles, and none are wearing masks.

Source C

'My hours of work at Mr Connell's mill were from a few minutes before half-past five in the morning till seven at night. Half an hour for breakfast. An hour for dinner. No baggin (tea).'

A factory worker quoted in the report of a Royal Commission to Parliament in 1833.

Source D

'In Willenhall the children are shamefully and most cruelly beaten with a horsewhip, strap, stick, hammer, handle, file or whatever tool is nearest to hand, or are struck with the clenched fist or kicked.'

Report of the Children's Employment Commission, 1843.

Source E

'Little boys and girls are seen here at work at the tip-punching machines, with their fingers in constant danger of being punched off. "They seldom lose the hand," said one of the owners, "it only takes off a finger at the first or second joint. Sheer carelessness."'

Children's Employment Commission, Third Report, 1864.

Source F

Women and children working down the mines.

Source G

'The racking noise of engines, the hell of sounds. The dragging, wearying monotony of the machine; the stifling heat; the unbroken noise; the need for constant action on the part of the workers; these render the place and the employment all but intolerable.'

Douglas Jerrold, a journalist, 1840.

Source H

'The factory folk are better clothed, better fed and better conducted than many other classes of working people. I found the mill a large building and very clean. The working rooms are spacious, well ventilated and lofty, kept at an even temperature and exceedingly clean. I observed great care in the boxing up of dangerous machinery and was told that accidents were very rare.'

A visitor to a mill in Bolton in 1844, reported in 'Chambers' Journal'.

Source I

'The youngest children in the mines are called trappers. Their job consists of sitting in a little hole by each door in the mine shafts. There they sit, with a string in their hands attached to the door, and pull it the moment they hear the carts at hand. They sit in the dark all the time the pit is worked.'

'Report on the Working Conditions in the Mines', 1842.

Questions

Section A

1 Describe the hardships of working in factories and mines at this time. Try and include the following:

long hours; harsh discipline; dangerous machinery; child labour; women workers; monotony; lack of independence.
   Make sure you use all of the sources as evidence to support your description.

Section B

2 Source H seems to give a different picture of working conditions from all of the rest of the sources. If you were a historian, would you:
   • believe Source H and assume that all of the other sources must be exaggerating;
   • assume Source H is just lies;
   • come to some other conclusion?
Explain your answer.

3 Sources C, D, E, F and I are from official inquiries set up by the government to investigate suspected bad working conditions. Do you think they are more reliable than the other sources in this unit? Explain your answer.

Factory Reform

As conditions in the factories got worse, a few individuals began try to introduce some safeguards. The campaigners were a very varied group. Some were even sympathetic factory owners such as **Sir Robert Peel** and **Robert Owen**. There were large public meetings, petitions to Parliament and letters to the newspapers. The main aim was to reduce people's working hours to ten hours a day.

By 1832 the leading figure in the **Ten–Hour Day Movement** was an MP, **Lord Anthony Ashley Cooper**, (later **Earl of Shaftesbury**), a Dorset landowner. He was a religious man, and the reports of factory conditions deeply moved him. He persuaded the government to set up a Royal Commission to look at working conditions in factories. When the commission reported, the government passed the **1833 Factory Act**.

This became the pattern. Campaigns outside Parliament forced governments to set up inquiries and the resulting reports led to Acts of Parliament. Shaftesbury's pressure led to Royal Commissions which in turn led to the **Mines Act of 1842** and the **Factory Act of 1844**. But there was still strong opposition to factory reform.

Source A

'Extreme hardship would be inflicted upon tens of thousands of families in Lancashire and Yorkshire, by a law fixing the hours at eight or even ten hours and *absolutely forbidding* the employment of any one child, whatever the circumstances, for a minute longer.'

The 'Leeds Mercury', December 1831.

Source B

'The 1833 Factory Act is dictated by the best intentions, but is a crude piece of legislation, calculated to harass the manufacturers by minute interference, while it secures for the children more leisure and less wages than their parents will approve.'

The 'Leeds Mercury', August 1833.

Source C

'Our only advantages consist in cheap machinery and low rates of interest. By restricting our mills to 69 hours a week, we have given up these advantages; by restricting them to 58, we not only annihilate them, but hand them over to the enemy.'

Robert Hyde Greg, 'The Factory Questions Considered', 1837.

Source D

'The exceeding easiness of cotton factory labour makes long hours of work practicable. With the exception of mule spinners, the work is merely that of watching the machinery and piecing together the threads that break. In a mill, the whole net profit is derived from the last hour. If the hours of work were reduced by one hour per day, the whole profit would be destroyed.'

Nassau Senior, an economist, 1837.

These were the main laws passed to improve conditions in the factories and mines.

1802 **Health and Morals of Apprentices Act** This law applied only to pauper children sent from workhouses to be apprentices in textile mills. It said that they could not be employed younger than 9 years old and could not work longer than 12 hours a day.

1819 **Factory Act** This law extended the 1802 Act to all children in cotton mills. It meant no work for children under 9 years old and set a 72 hour maximum week for children aged between 9 and 16. Unfortunately, there was no method of inspecting factories to enforce this law.

1833 **Althorp's Factory Act** This was the first effective legislation. It applied to the whole textile industry except lace and silk making. It banned work for children under 9 and set a maximum 48 hour week for 9 to 13 year olds, with an additional 2 hours per day of compulsory schooling. Children aged 13 to 16 could work no more than 69 hours per week and night work was banned for those under 18. Four factory inspectors were appointed to enforce this law. Four were not enough, but the inspectorate grew in size and efficiency over the years.

1842 **Mines and Collieries Act** This Act only controlled working conditions in the mines. It outlawed the employment of women and children under 10 years old underground. It also said that winding gear should not be entrusted to children less than 15. Mines inspectors were appointed to enforce the law.

1844 **Graham's Factory Act** This Act also applied to the whole of the textile industry except silk and lace. It reduced the minimum age for child labour to 8 years, and set a 6½ hour maximum working day, with half a day schooling, for 8 to 13 year olds. No women and no boys under 18 were to work more than 12 hours a day. All dangerous machinery was to be fenced in.

1847 **Fielden's Factory Act** This law finally achieved a 10 hour maximum working day for women and children under 18. But employers still kept factories open from about 5.30 a.m. until 8.30 p.m. and worked the women and children in relays so that they could keep the men working the whole time.

1850 **Grey's Factory Act** The maximum working day for women and children was extended to 10½ hours in exchange for an agreement that these must be between 6.00 a.m. and 6.00 p.m. Factories could employ men for these 12 hours only which, with 1½ hours of meal breaks, meant almost a 10-hour day in the cotton industry.

Source E

A factory inspector checking the ages of child workers. Do you think that the artist was a factory reform campaigner?

Questions

Section A

1 Read the details of the laws passed between 1802 and 1850 to control working conditions. Draw a graph, based on the outline below, to show the amount of progress made at each stage. Acts which you think made big improvements must make bigger jumps up your graph than less important Acts.

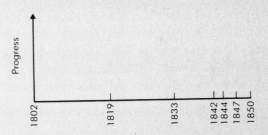

2 Write an explanation to go with your graph. You must explain why you consider some of the laws more important than others.

Section B

3 Consider this list of problems for factory workers:
● long hours for adults
● long hours for children
● dangerous machinery

Which of these problems would seem the most important to:
a Lord Shaftesbury?
b a father who was a machine operator, whose children also worked in the same factory?
c a factory owner?

Give reasons for your answers.

Living Conditions in Industrial Towns

During the Industrial Revolution, the population of the towns grew too fast for the authorities to cope. In 1821 Britain had 1 million houses; by 1851 there were 2¼ million. But this wasn't enough. The houses that were built were cheap and overcrowded. They usually didn't have piped water supplies, drains or sewers. Water came to stand-pipes in the street direct from the local rivers. Sewage was often pumped untreated into the same rivers. There was no proper system of refuse disposal.

The result was widespread disease. **Typhoid** was spread in infected water. **Typhus fever** was spread by lice and **tuberculosis** by bacteria coughed into the air by infected people – both spreading quickly in the overcrowded streets and houses. They were killer diseases. Life expectancy was very low. In 1831 **cholera** appeared for the first time in Britain. There were further outbreaks in 1838, 1848, and 1854. Cholera was the a terrible problem in nineteenth-century towns, killing hundreds of thousands of people.

Source A

'The one-storey houses have ill-fitting planks and broken windows. The outside walls have no cavities to keep out the wet and the cold. The moisture creeps up the walls, making them black and damp. Foundations are weak, so that the walls often crack. Roofs often leak, and many of the doors and windows do not fit.'

Alexis de Tocqueville, a French visitor to Manchester in 1835.

Source B

Source C

	1801	1851
Birmingham	71,000	233,000
Bradford	17,000	104,000
Glasgow	77,000	345,000
Liverpool	82,000	376,000
London	957,000	2,362,000

Population of British towns.

Source D

'The working classes of Liverpool numbered 160,000 people at that time. Only half lived in acceptable houses facing the street, 22,158 lived in 6,915 cellars (underneath other people's houses).'

Census Report, 1841.

Source E

'In a cellar in Liverpool, I found a mother and her grown-up daughters sleeping in a bed of straw on the ground in the corner of the cellar. In the other corner, three sailors had their bed. I have met upwards of forty people sleeping in the same room.'

Edwin Chadwick, a campaigner for better living conditions, 1842.

A picture from the 'Illustrated London News', 1853. You can clearly see the overcrowding. You have to use your judgement about the damp and poor ventilation.

Source F

'Each yard is furnished with a privy [toilet], and the tenant usually added a pigsty and a midden [dunghill]. The yard is 13 feet long by 11 feet wide, (about 4 metres by 3.5 metres). Into the midden the contents of the privy drain through a hole. The household rubbish would have been added too. The matter thus collected is removed twice a year.'

'Commission on the State of Large Towns', 1844.

Source G

'The water is turned on a certain number of hours during the day, four hours perhaps; the poor go to the tap for it; it is constantly running; each person fetches as much as they have pans to receive; but they have not many of these and they are frequently out of water. It is not sufficient for washing or anything of that kind.'

A report on conditions in Liverpool in the 1840s.

Source H

People queuing for water in Bethnal Green, London in 1863.

Source I

THE WATER THAT JOHN DRINKS.

This is the water that John drinks.

This is the Thames with its cento of stink,
That supplies the water that John drinks.

These are the fish that float in the ink-
-y stream of the Thames with its cento of stink,
That supplies the water that John drinks

This is the sewer, from cesspool and sink,
That feeds the fish that float in the ink-
-y stream of the Thames with its cento of stink,
That supplies the water that John drinks.

A comment by 'Punch' on the quality of London's drinking water, which often came from the Thames — where much of London's sewage went.

Questions

Section A

1 Use the information in this unit to describe the living conditions of the poor in industrial towns at this time.

Section B

2 In your answer to question 1 above, you may have just accepted all of the information in all of the sources as **true**. However, historians would not do this. They would trust some sources more than others. Say why you might, or might not, trust the following:

a Source A, a foreign visitor describing what he saw on his visit to Manchester.

b Sources D and F, extracts from official government reports.

c Sources B and I, illustrations from magazines.

d Source E, a quotation from a man campaigning to get improvements in living conditions.

3 Source H is a picture. We know nothing about the artist. We don't know if he or she was an expert on the living conditions of the poor or whether he or she was biased. Yet we have good reason to trust the picture of the way that the poor got their water. The reason is contained in this unit. What is it? Explain your answer.

Public Health Reform

Many people were very concerned about the living conditions of the poor in nineteenth century towns. But little was done about the problem before 1850.

The cholera epidemic of 1831–2 provoked some action. Thirty thousand people died within a year. The government set up the first Boards of Health to find ways to stop the disease. Disease increased poverty, because it stopped people working. More poverty increased the rates (local taxes) that people paid to help the poor. Besides, disease didn't always respect social boundaries. Epidemics which started in the slums sometimes spread among the wealthy. But as soon as the epidemic passed, these Boards of Health were disbanded.

It was **Edwin Chadwick** who did most to campaign for reform. In 1838, he started a national inquiry, which led to the **Report on the Sanitary Conditions of the Labouring Population of Great Britain** (1842). The Report had a big impact upon public opinion. It included Chadwick's ideas for solving many of the public health problems of the towns, such as 'arterial water supply systems' which would bring fresh piped water into towns and then use the excess to flush refuse and sewage away down drains and sewers. The Report argued that the problem could no longer be left to local councils to solve. They didn't have the power or the funds to start such schemes. If councils did suggest improvements, local ratepayers complained that they were too expensive for the rates to bear.

Source B

'The country is sick of centralisation, of Commissions, of inquiries. The people want to be left to manage their own affairs. They do not want Parliament to be so paternal as it wishes to be – interfering in everbody's business and, like all who interfere, not doing its own so well.'

George Hudson MP, 1847.

Source C

'I object also to the Board of Health Commissioners being salaried. If they have not the patriotism to give their services for the good of the country, they are utterly unworthy of so important a trust.'

Colonel Sibthorp, MP for Lincoln, objecting to spending public money on the Public Health Act in 1847.

Source A

A cartoon from 'Punch' showing 'King Bumble' as the town councils, lazy and deaf to the pleas of the poor.

But the government refused to act. Why was progress so slow? One reason was that many people objected to public health reforms. For example the water carriers who feared they would be put out of business, or the poor people who did not want to get rid of the piggeries in their back yards. People who thought like this became known as the 'dirty party'. Their attitude to government is known as *laissez-faire*. They believed that people should be left alone to run their own lives and that the government should interfere as little as possible.

It eventually took another cholera epidemic in 1848, when about 250,000 people died, to stir Parliament to action. The **Public Health Act of 1848** was passed. This Act was just what the country needed. It set up a Central Board of Health for a period of five years to advise local Boards of Health wherever towns set them up. Soon there were almost 200 local boards covering about 2 million people. They set about cleaning streets, inspecting all new house-building and increasing piped water supplies and sewers. They could charge rates to cover the cost of these improvements. In some towns, they were very active. In Macclesfield, the death rate fell from 43 per thousand in 1847 to 26 per thousand by 1856.

But the Central Board was unpopular, and the latest cholera epidemic had died down. The board was renewed in 1853 but abolished in 1858. It wasn't until 1875 that a new Public Health Act was passed to ensure better living conditions in the towns.

Source D

THE "SILENT HIGHWAY"-MAN.

Source E

'We prefer to take our chance with the cholera than be bullied into health. There is nothing a man hates so much as being cleansed against his will or having his floor swept, his halls whitewashed, his dungheaps cleared away and his thatch forced to give way to slate.'

The 'Times', 1854.

Questions

Section A

1 Draw a time-line and place on it Britain's major cholera outbreaks (1831, 1838, 1848 and 1854). Then add the setting up of the **first** public health boards; Chadwick's national inquiry into public health; and the passing of the Public Health Act and its abolition.

2 Use your time-line from question 1 to explain the story of public health reform from 1800 to 1854.

Section B

3 The town of Melchester has a serious public health problem. It has thousands of unhealthy, overcrowded homes and a death rate of 45 per thousand. One set of private contractors brings in its water supply in watercarts; another contractor collects all the sewage, also in carts. A cholera epidemic has broken out in a nearby town. The local Board of Health has suggested building an arterial water system. How would all the people concerned react to this?

This cartoon highlights the problem in nineteenth-century towns. People either had to spend money on improvements, or pay with their lives.

Working-Class Reactions (1): Violence

Working people did not always just stand by and accept the changes caused by the Industrial Revolution. Their reactions varied. The next three units describe those reactions. This unit concentrates on the times when that reaction was violent. The two best known examples are **Luddism** and the **Swing Riots**.

The Luddites

New machinery was putting hand loom weavers out of work in the early nineteenth century. In Nottinghamshire and Derbyshire wide looms and shearing frames were being used to make broad strips of cloth which could be cut up and sewn into tubes to make socks and stockings. These were of poorer quality than the ones made on the old narrow frames but cheaper and needed fewer weavers. Even worse for the workers in Lancashire, Cheshire and Yorkshire, were the new steam-powered looms. Power looms had been invented long before but they were just becoming common. These machines didn't require such skilled workers and could be used only in factories. They didn't just reduce the need for hand-loom weavers, they replaced them.

There were also high food prices between 1810 and 1814 and a depression in industry after 1815 which reduced jobs and wages. These things made the problems of the hand-loom weavers worse. Between 1811 and 1813, and again in 1816, the weavers started to hit out at the most obvious causes of their problems – the machines and the owners. Factories were broken into, machines were smashed, and owners were attacked. In 1812 a factory owner was killed near Huddersfield, and a factory was burned down in Wigan. Five weavers were killed when guns were used to stop an attack on a factory in Middleton in Lancashire.

Stories spread about a leader of these machine breakers called **Ned Ludd**, sometimes 'Captain' or 'King' Ludd. It was even said that he would lead a general rising of workers and overthrow the government. Machine breaking was made a crime punishable by death. Seventeen men were executed after Luddite trials at York in 1812. Troops were moved into troubled areas. Ned Ludd was almost certainly a mythical figure, and there was no national organisation. The Luddites frightened many people with their protests, but it was a passing phase. After 1820, when the depression lifted, nothing more was heard of them.

Source A

'Sir,
Information has just been given in that you are the owner of those hateful shearing frames. I was asked by my men to write to you and give you notice that you should pull them down. You will take note that if they are not taken down by the end of next week, I will send one of my lieutenants with at least 300 men to destroy them. If you give us the trouble of coming so far, we will increase your misfortune by burning your house down to ashes. And if you dare fire on any of my men, they have orders to murder you and burn all your housing.

Ludd'

A letter sent to Frederick Smith, a factory owner in Huddersfield, in 1812.

Source B

December 23, 1811.

WHEREAS

A most violent Attack was made about 8 o'clock last Night, on the House of Mr. JOHN BRENTNALL, at LOCKO GRANGE, in the County of Derby, by Eight or more Persons, two of whom with their Faces blacked & armed with Pistols, entered the House, but in consequence of the spirited Resistance of the Family, retired without effecting their villainous purposes.

One of the Men about five feet nine inches high and broad set, is supposed to have his Head, Face, and Neck much injured in a struggle; and another Man about six feet high is supposed to be wounded by a Bill Hook; the other Men who did not enter the House, as far as could be distinguished from the darkness of the night, appeared to be above the common size.

A REWARD OF

FIFTY POUNDS

Has been offered by his Royal Highness the Prince Regent on the Conviction of EACH PERSON concerned in any Outrages of the above nature, and a free Pardon in case the Person giving such information as may lead to the Conviction shall be liable to be prosecuted for the same.

(J. Drewry, Printer, Derby.)

This poster was published after a Luddite attack on a local employer. You can tell how seriously the authorities treated the attacks by the size of the reward offered.

The Swing Riots

Machine breaking broke out again during rioting by farm workers in southern England in 1830. Again there was talk of a leader, **'Captain Swing'**, though once more he didn't really exist.

Farming was in a depression. Wages were low, and work was in short supply. When the 1830 harvest failed, there was less food and less work. Riots broke out among labourers in Kent and spread. Eventually there were troubles in twenty-two counties. The labourers burned hay ricks, damaged buildings and attacked machinery. Their favourite targets were the steam-powered threshing machines which reduced the work for men. A total of 387 threshing machines were destroyed. Farmers were also attacked as a protest against low wages, but there was only one death. Again the government reacted harshly. Nine rioters were hanged, 457 transported and over 400 imprisoned.

Causes and Consequences

The Industrial Revolution brought rapid changes to people's lives. We are now used to rapid change, but at first it frightened people. Working people did not have the vote, so they could not rely on the government to make things better. They did not have powerful trade unions to turn to. When high food prices and low wages in the depressed 1810s and 1820s made things worse, they hit out. However machine breaking was not a very successful response to industrialisation. The Luddites and Swing Rioters achieved very little in the long run.

Source C

STATE OF THE COUNTRY.

A cartoon of 1830. You can see landowners on the right, debating what to do; farmers in the centre, trying to guard their property; and labourers on the left burning barns and breaking machinery.

Questions

Section A

1 Copy out the following sentences, re-arranging the 'tails' so that each goes with the right 'head'.

Heads	Tails
a Luddite protests occurred	shearing frames and power looms.
b The Swing Riots took place	in the years 1811–13 and 1816.
c The Luddites were	farm labourers.
d The Swing rioters were	threshing machines.
e The Luddites resented	hand loom weavers.
f The Swing rioters resented	in 1830.

Section B

2 a Why did Luddism break out in 1812, not in 1802 or 1822?
  b Why did the Swing Riots take place in 1830 not in 1832?

3 Did the machine breaking in Nottinghamshire, Kent and Lancashire all have the same causes, or different ones?

4 Why did the machine breakers turn to violence to solve their problems rather than finding peaceful solutions?

5 'Machine breaking in the Industrial Revolution did not have just one cause, but lots of causes.' Do you agree or disagree? Give reasons for your answer.

Working Class Reactions (2): Trade Unions

As the Industrial Revolution developed, it was the **unskilled workers** who needed help most. Their wages were lower. They were easily replaced by child labour. They were the ones who faced the worst working conditions and were most threatened by the new machines. But they failed to organise successful trade unions before 1850.

One reason was the **Combination Acts**. These laws banned all 'combinations' or trade unions. They had been passed in 1799 and 1800 when Britain was at war with France. The government had thought that unions would harm the economy and weaken the war effort. The Combination Acts were not repealed until 1824.

As soon as workers got the freedom to set up unions, they rushed at the chance with high hopes. They tended to form **national** unions, representing all of the workers in a trade. In 1829, for example, John Doherty formed the Grand General Union of Spinners. They even tried to combine **all** trades into one single union. Doherty formed the National Association for the Protection of Labour in 1830. It had 100,000 members from textiles, mining, pottery and twenty other trades.

But all of the large unions created in this period failed. We can see the reasons for this in the history of the largest of them all, the **Grand National Consolidated Trades Union (GNCTU)**.

The GNCTU was formed in 1834 by **Robert Owen**. Small unions were combined to form one union for all workers. By June 1834 it claimed to have 500,000 members each paying 1 shilling (5p) per week. He wrote, 'The design of the union is in the first instance to increase wages and to cut down the hours of labour. But the great and final object of it must be to set up a different order of things which will give the working classes more say.'

A general strike of all workers for one month was planned for 1834. It was assumed that this 'sacred month' would force the government and the employers to give in to the demands of the workers. But the sacred month never happened, and by 1835 the GNCTU had collapsed, like all the others.

One reason was that such unions were **too large**. Slow communications and low levels of literacy amongst members made it impossible to get everyone to agree to a

Source A

'The greater part of the evidence against us was put into the mouths of the witnesses by the judge. He told them that if such societies were allowed to exist, it would ruin masters, stagnate trade and destroy property.'

George Loveless, leader of the Tolpuddle Martyrs, 1838.

Source B

'The labouring population from one end of the kingdom to the other has been roused and angered. All this means nothing to Parliament. MPs say that it was necessary to terrify the working classes.'

J. A. Roebuck MP, 1835.

Source C

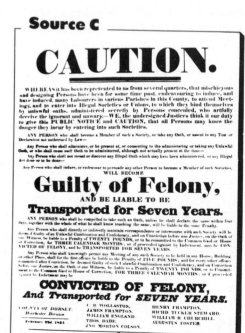

This poster appeared soon after the trial of the Tolpuddle Martyrs.

common policy and then carry it out together. Some unions refused to support other trades. The clothiers, potters, spinners and builders never joined the GNCTU; they didn't want to have anything to do with other people's disputes. Some members were also too poor to pay the subscriptions necessary to run such a large union.

Source D

Yes Gentlemen, these is my principles, — no K . . g, — no L . . ds, — no Parsons, — no Police, — no Taxes.

A cartoon of a union meeting from 1830. The union leader is saying, 'Yes gentlemen these is my principles, No K . . g, No L . . . s, No parsons, No Police, No Taxes, ...'.

Another reason was that the unions were **too radical**. Neither employers nor the government could afford to stand by and watch the workers take over. The employers decided to act. In Derby in 1834 they began to force their workers to sign 'the document' which said:

'We, the undersigned, do hereby declare that we are not members of a trade union; that we do not and will not pay towards the support of any such association.'

Fifteen hundred workers who refused to sign were locked out of work. Employers had the funds to close factories and let poverty drive the workers back.

The **government** also acted against the unions. In 1833 forty farm labourers from Tolpuddle in Dorset, led by George Loveless, set up a local branch of the GNCTU. As was usual, new members were sworn in by making an oath of loyalty to the union. But local magistrates were told by the government to arrest the leaders for 'administering illegal oaths'. This was a charge which was meant to be used against sailors plotting a mutiny. But the six leaders were found guilty and in 1834 were sentenced to seven years transportation. The warning to other workers was clear. Working people began to desert the GNCTU in large numbers and it collapsed in 1835. Only small local groups continued. Eventually, after 1850, these local groups combined to form many of the unions which still exist today.

Questions

Section A

1 Draw a time-line from 1790 to 1850 and mark on it the key events of the history of trade unions in this period.

2 Write one paragraph which describes these events. Make sure you mention every event on your time-line.

3 a Find in the text Robert Owen's description of the aims of the GNCTU. Re-write his description in your own words.
  b Why was there a need for workers to have an organisation with these aims?

Section B

4 Look at Sources A, B and C. Do they support the view that the government helped to cause the failure of trades unions in this period?

5 Are the following causes of the failure of trade unions in this period? Say 'yes' or 'no' to each and explain your answers.

  a The unions were too ambitious and radical.
  b The employers opposed the unions.

6 Is cause **a** in question 5 in any way connected to cause **b**?

7 Historians usually find that there are lots of causes for events in history and that these causes are often linked or connected to each other. Explain why trade unions failed in this period, using the following list of causes. Whenever you can, show how the causes are linked or connected:
  ● the unions were too ambitious and radical
  ● the government opposed them
  ● the employers opposed them
  ● the unions were too large
  ● poor communications
  ● weak finances
  ● splits among the workers

117

Working Class Reactions (3): Chartism

Working people needed the help of Parliament to solve their problems. New laws were needed to improve wages, food prices, working conditions and housing. But during the Industrial Revolution very few working people had the vote. In the 1830s and 1840s there was an attempt to change this. Working people tried to persuade Parliament to accept six changes to the system for electing MPs. These 'Six Points' made up the **People's Charter**. (Source A). The Six Points were intended to give working people control of Parliament

The supporters of the Charter, known as the Chartists, tried several ways of getting Parliament to accept their demands. Some of them wanted to take over the country by force and then put the Charter into practice. In 1839, for example, there was a Chartist uprising in Newport, Wales.

Source A

The Six Points of the People's Charter

1 *A vote* for every man of at least 21 years of age.

2 A *secret ballot* to protect the elector as he votes.

3 *No property qualification* for members of parliament, thus enabling the return of the man of their choice, be he rich or poor.

4 *Payment of members*, thus enabling a working man to serve.

5 *Equal constituencies*, to get fair representation for everyone.

6 *Annual Parliaments*, so members, when elected for a year only, would not be able to betray their constituents as now.

A summary of the People's Charter taken from a poster of the time.

Source B

'At least 8,000 men were in the attack, many of them armed. The design of the leaders was to raise rebellion throughout Wales until the people of England should rise. The people marched to the Westgate Hotel where the JPs and about forty soldiers were. The soldiers fired, with ease and security, upon the people who had first broken and fired into the windows. About thirty of the people are known to have been killed.'

Source C

'The parcel of people I saw had guns, sticks etc.; the sticks had iron points. I did not see many with guns. They asked for the prisoners, then a rush was made. Then I heard firing and I took to my heels.'

Edward Patton, a Newport carpenter, 1839.

Source D

'Thirty soldiers were ordered to guard the Westgate Hotel in which a number of Chartists were imprisoned. A Chartist shouted "Give up the prisoners." Six Chartists entered the lobby of the hotel and opened fire. The shutters of the hotel were flung back, and the soldiers fired. Between ten and twenty Chartists were killed. The rest fled.'

The Mayor of Newport, 1989.

Source E

An artist's impression of the Newport Uprising of 1839.

Report in 'The Charter', 17 November 1839.

Other Chartists wanted to **persuade** Parliament. In 1839, 1842 and 1848 huge petitions were presented to Parliament. In 1848 there was a big rally in London to take the final petition, with its 5 million signatures, to Parliament. But the petition was found to be full of forgeries. Among the names were 'Pug Nose', 'Queen Victoria' and, several times, 'The Duke of Wellington'. It was rejected: in fact the Charter was never adopted by Parliament. The Chartists were no more successful than the Luddites or the early trade unionists in controlling the impact of the Industrial Revolution on their lives

Source F

'The Kennington Common meeting has ended in complete failure. About 15,000 people met in good order. O'Connor, the Chartist leader, looked pale and frightened. He was told that the meeting could go ahead but that no marchers would be allowed to pass over the bridges to Parliament. O'Connor advised the crowd to go home.'

Lord John Russell, the Prime Minister, 10 April 1848.

Source G

The Chartist rally at Kennington Common, London in 1848.

Source H

The Kennington Common meeting described in a 'Punch' cartoon. The Duke of Wellington appears nine times in the crowd!

Questions

Section A

1 Fill in the gaps in this paragraph.

The aim of the Chartists was to get the . . . . . adopted. This contained the . . . . . which were aimed at getting control of . . . . in the hands of the . . . . . . class. Sometimes the Chartists tried to . . . . . . the Charter on the government; sometimes they tried to . . . . . . them. But the Charter was never adopted. The Chartist movement ended in ridicule in . . . .

Section B

2 Look at Sources B, C, D and E. For each source in turn answer the following questions.

   a Does this source tell me anything the others don't?
   b Does this source repeat anything in the other sources?
   c Does this source contradict anything in the other sources?

3 What do you think happened at the Westgate Hotel (Source D)?

4 Historians always try to look at as many sources as possible before deciding what they think happened. Why?

5 Sources F, G and H all give different impressions of the Kennington Common meeting. Describe the impression each one gives.

6 'Sources F, G and H all give different impressions. They are all therefore useless. Historians should ignore them.' Do you agree? Explain your answer.

Population

We estimate the population of Britain to have been about 7 million in 1750. There was no official census until 1801, when a total of 10.5 million was recorded. There has been a census taken every ten years ever since (except during the Second World War). By 1850 the number of people living in Britain had doubled to 20.8 million. So the population was rising extremely quickly during the Industrial Revolution. Why was this?

The Causes of Population Increase

Some historians argue that, because people were living longer, the **death rate** went down. They say that agricultural improvements helped by keeping food plentiful and prices low most of the time. They also suggest that industrial changes helped by increasing the number of jobs and providing cheap clothes and household goods to improve the quality of life. Some historians also say that the growth of towns helped too. They say that in the towns people benefited from brick houses with tiled roofs, water supplies and drains. Towns often had hospitals for the sick. Epidemics of diseases like the bubonic plague and scarlet fever declined in the eighteenth century. But there is some doubt whether living conditions really did improve enough to have caused the population to rise so quickly (see page 110).

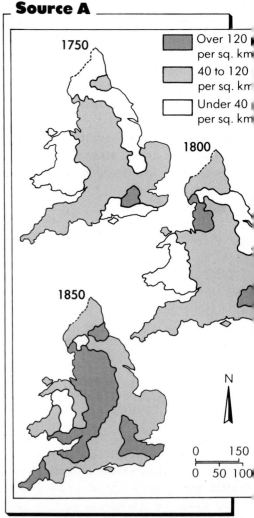

Source A

	Over 120 per sq. km
	40 to 120 per sq. km
	Under 40 per sq. km

1750

1800

1850

N

0   150
0   50 100

The distribution of population. These maps can be used to see where the population was growing fastest.

*This graph shows the **size** of the population during the Industrial Revolution. By looking at the steepness of the curve, you can also see how the **rate** of population growth changed.*

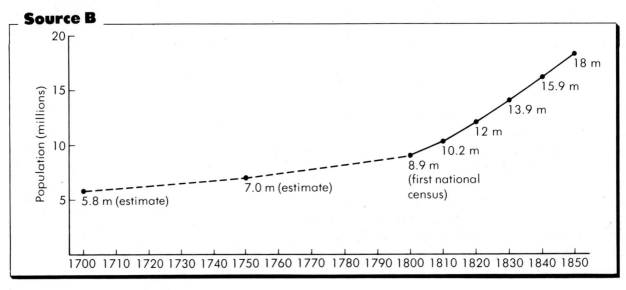

Source B

5.8 m (estimate)

7.0 m (estimate)

8.9 m (first national census)

10.2 m

12 m

13.9 m

15.9 m

18 m

Other historians argue that the population was rising because people were having more children – the **birth rate** was going up. They say that industrial changes helped by providing more jobs. When people feel confident of staying in work, they are more likely to have more children. Many of the jobs created in factories during the Industrial Revolution didn't need long apprenticeships. So men could earn full wages earlier, marry earlier and have children sooner. In an age when contraception was not very efficient, the earlier couples married, the more children they were likely to have. Before the Industrial Revolution, too many children had always brought the fear of poverty; children were expensive to feed. But many of the new jobs in industry were for children. Child labour in the factories meant that children could earn their keep sooner, and this may have encouraged large families. From 1795 onwards, poor families in parts of the country could get financial help from the poor law under the Speenhamland System. The more children they had, the more money they got. Factors like these may have encouraged people to have more children, but this is very difficult to prove.

Regional variations

The population of every county in England rose between 1750 and 1850, but the **rate** of population increase was not evenly spread. Industrial areas, especially mining and textile areas, grew faster than other areas. Towns grew faster than the countryside. This was partly because the changes in the birth rate and death rate were greatest in these areas. But it was also partly because people moved, or **migrated** to these places from other areas in search of jobs.

Effects of Population Growth

We have seen how changes in industry, agriculture and transport may have helped to cause the increase in population. The Industrial Revolution was one of the causes of population increase. But the rise in population also led to changes. More people meant more workers and customers for industry and farmers. Plenty of workers meant that employers didn't have to pay such high wages to attract labour. Plenty of customers meant that businesspeople and farmers could charge higher prices for their produce. The population growth therefore helped keep wages low and prices high for industry and agriculture. So it was one of the causes of the success of the Industrial Revolution.

Questions

Section A

1 Look at Source A. Use an atlas to find out the names of the areas which grew as the population increased during the Industrial Revolution.

2 List the reasons why some historians think the death rate went down between 1750 and 1850.

3 List the reasons why some historians think the birth rate went up between 1750 and 1850.

Section B

4 Are all the causes you listed in your answers to questions 2 and 3 equally important?

5 a What do you think were the two main causes of the increase in population from 1750 to 1850? (Think about information you have gained from other units in the book.)
  b Explain why you have chosen these two.

6 The diagram below shows one causal link between the changes in industry, agriculture and population. Copy the diagram into your book and then try to draw in as many other causal links as you can.

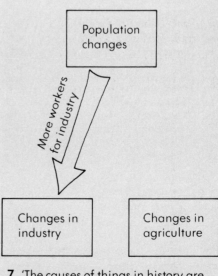

7 'The causes of things in history are complicated.' Use your answers to the questions above to explain this statement.

Acknowledgements

The authors and publishers would like to thank the following for permission to reproduce photographs on the pages indicated:

Ashmolean Museum: pp. 27 (*right*), 33, 36 and 37
Bridgeman Art Library (private collection): p. 48 (*top right*)
British Library: pp. 21, 28, 38, 39, 40 (*middle*), 41, 42, 43 (*top*), 44 (*left*), 54 and 87
British Museum: pp. 17, 25, 40 (*lower*) and 56 (*top and lower*)
British Waterways Board: p. 94
Dr R A Buchanan: p. 79 (*top*)
Derby Local Studies Library: p. 78 (*lower right*)
Derbyshire Archaeological Society: p. 72 (*top*)
Eling Tide Mill: p. 79 (*middle*)
Mary Evans Picture Library: pp. 29 (*lower right*), 69 (*lower*), 72 (*lower*), 84 (*lower*), 85, 88 (*middle and lower*), 93 (*top left*), 106, 111 (*left*) and 119 (*lower*)
J R Freeman: pp. 22 and 35
Hampshire County Library: p. 93 (*top right*)
H M The Queen: p. 119 (*lower*)
Hulton-Deutsch: pp. 9, 46 (*top*), 57, 80, 93 (*middle and lower left*), 113 and 117
Illustrated London News Picture Library: pp. 86 (*lower left*) and 110
Institute of Agricultural History and Museum of English Rural Life: p. 67
Ironbridge Gorge Museum Trust: pp. 76 and 77
Manchester City Art Gallery: p. 11
Mansell Collection: pp. 45, 46 (*lower right*), 51, 55, 56 (*middle*), 60, 86 (*top right*), 90, 96, 101, 107, 109, 115 and 118
National Portrait Gallery: p. 27 (*top left*)
National Railway Museum: p. 105 (*lower right*)
Prado, Madrid/Bridgeman Art Library: p. 5
Punch Publications: pp. 99, 105 (*top*) and 112
Ann Ronan Picture Library: pp. 13, 78 (*middle left*) and 104

Tichborne Park, Hampshire/Bridgeman Art Library: p. 63
Trade Union Congress: p. 16
The Trustees of the Wedgwood Museum: pp. 88 (*top right*) and 89

Thanks are also due to David & Charles for permission to reproduce the photograph on page 97 which is taken from *British Canals: an Illustrated History* by Charles Hadfield.

The authors and publishers would also like to thank the following for permission to reproduce copyright material:

B. T. Batsford Ltd for permission to reproduce the graphs on p. 64, which originally appeared in: *The Agricultural Revolution 1750–1880* by J. D. Chambers and G. E. Mingay
Hampshire County Library for the extracts from *Sadler's Directory of Hampshire*, p. 93
Methuen Ltd for the population maps on p. 120
Ordnance Survey © Crown Copyright for the map on p. 100, and for the map on p. 103 which was reproduced from the 1870 Ordnance Survey map
Mr Rex Russell for the enclosure map of Scartho on p. 64
The Southern Regional Examinations Board and the Southern Examining Group for permission to reproduce material originally used in examination papers.

Every effort has been made to trace all copyright holders, but if any have been inadvertently overlooked the publishers will be pleased to make the necessary arrangement at the first opportunity.

Details of written sources

In some sources the wording or sentence structure has been simplified to make sure that the source is accessible.

Unit 1.2
Sources A, C and E: S. J. Houston, *James I*, Longman, 1973
Sources B and D: David Harris Willson, *King James VI and I*, Jonathan Cape, 1956

Unit 1.3
Source A: Keith Thomas, *Religion and the Decline of Magic*, Weidenfeld and Nicolson, 1971
Source B: Christopher Hill, *Antichrist in Seventeenth Century England*, Oxford University Press, 1971

Unit 1.5
Sources A, B and C: Lawrence Stone, *The Family, Sex and Marriage in England, 1500–1800*, Penguin, 1979
Source E: Alan Macfarlane (ed.), *The Diary of Ralph Josselin*, British Academy, 1956

Unit 1.8
Source B: C. R. N. Routh, *They Saw it Happen 1485–1688*, Basil Blackwell, 1956

Unit 1.14
Source A: Peter Young, *Oliver Cromwell*, Severn House, 1976
Source B: R. Potter and G. A. Embleton, *The English Civil War*, Almark, 1973

Unit 1.15
Source B: John Cruso, *Militarie Instructions for the Cavalry*, Reprinted by The Roundwood Press, 1972
Source C: Roy Sherwood, *Civil Strife in the Midlands 1642–1651*, Phillimore, 1974

Unit 1.17
Source B: A. S. P. Woodhouse (ed.), *Puritanism and Liberty*, Dent, 1938

Unit 1.20
Source D: Anne Everit Green (ed.), *Calendar of State Papers, Domestic Series 1653–54*, HMSO, 1857–1947

Unit 1.22
Sources A & E: A. F. Scott (ed.), *Everyone a Witness: The Stuart Age*, White Lion Publishers, 1974
Source D: Alan Macfarlane, 'Witchcraft' in *History of the English Speaking Peoples*, Purnell, 1970

Unit 1.25
Source A: Godfrey Davis, *The Restoration of Charles II*, Oxford University Press, 1955

Unit 1.26
Boxed Text: Robert Latham and William Matthews (eds.), *Diary of Samuel Pepys, Vol. 1–9*, Bell and Hyman, 1971–83

Unit 1.27
Source B: Schools Council History Project, *Medicine Through Time II*, Holmes Macdougall, 1976
Source D: Latham and Matthews, *Diary of Samuel Pepys*

Unit 1.28
Source D: Latham and Matthews, *Diary of Samuel Pepys*

Unit 2.3
Source A: J. Steven Watson, *The Reign of George III*, Oxford University Press, 1960
Source B: J. Robottom, *A Social and Economic History of Industrial Britain*, Longman, 1986

Unit 2.4
Source B: Dorothy Thompson, *The British People 1760–1902*, Heinemann Educational, 1969
Source C: L. W. Cowie, *Industrial Evolution, 1750 to the Present Day*, Nelson, 1975
Source D: D. P. Titley, *Machines, Money and Men*, Hart-Davis, 1977
Source E: P. F. Speed, *History through Maps and Diagrams: The Industrial Revolution to Present-Day Britain*, Arnold-Wheaton, 1985

Unit 2.6
Source D: R. Rundle, *Britain's Economic and Social Development*, Hodder and Stoughton, 1973

Unit 2.7
Source B: Phyllis Deane, *The First Industrial Revolution*, Cambridge University Press, 1965

Unit 2.8
Sources A, C, D and I: Neil Cossons and Barrie Trinder, *Iron Bridge: Symbol of the Industrial Revolution*, Moonraker Press, 1979

Unit 2.10
Source A: Asa Briggs, *The Age of Improvement*, Longman, 1959
Source B: C. Harvie, *The Industrial Revolution*, Open University Press, 1972
Source C: John Wilkes, *United Kingdom*, Cambridge University Press, 1984

Unit 2.12
Source C: R. J. Cootes, *Britain Since 1700*, Longman, 1968
Source D: D. P. Titley, *Machines, Money and Men*
Source E: C. P. Hill, *British Economic and Social History 1900–75*, Edward Arnold, 1977
Source F: J. Addy, *A Coal and Iron Community in the Industrial Revolution*, Longman, 1969
Source H: N. Buxton, *The Economic Development of the British Coal Industry*, Batsford, 1978
Source I: J. Thurkettle, *An Outline of the Social and Economic History of Britain 1066–1956*, Pergamon Press, 1968

Unit 2.13
Source C: Neil Buxton, *Economic Development of the British Coal Industry*
Source D: W. O. Skeat, *George Stephenson: The Engineer and his Letters*, Institute of Engineers, 1973
Sources E & H: Hunter Davies, *George Stephenson: A Biographical Study*, Weidenfeld & Nicolson, 1975

Unit 2.15
Source C: C. McNab and R. Mackenzie, *From Waterloo to the Great Exhibition*, Oliver and Boyd, 1982

Unit 2.18

Source C: P. F. Speed, *The Growth of the British Economy 1700–1850,* Arnold Wheaton, 1980

Source E: C. Hadfield, *British Canals: An Illustrated History,* David & Charles, 1984

Unit 2.19

Source A: J. Simmons, *The Railways of Britain: an Historical Introduction,* Macmillan, 1968

Source B: J. R. Francis, *History of the English Railway,* Longman, Brown & Green, 1851

Source C: H. Perkin, *Age of The Railway,* David & Charles, 1970

Source D: L. Hartley and J. Nichol, *The Industrial Revolution,* Basil Blackwell, 1975

Unit 2.20

Sources C, D and F: Terry Coleman, *The Railway Navvies,* Penguin, 1968

Source E: W. R. Mitchell and D. Joy, *Settle to Carlisle: A Railway over the Pennines,* Dalesman, 1973

Unit 2.23

Sources A & G: Quoted in L. Hartley and J. Nichol, *The Industrial Revolution*

Source E: J. Robottom, *A Social and Economic History of Industrial Britain*

Sources B, C H and I: Quoted in: Philip Sauvain, *British Economic and Social History 1700–1830,* Stanley Thornes, 1987

Unit 2.24

Sources A–D: Quoted in Howard Martin, *Britain Since 1800: Towards the Welfare State,* Macmillan Education, 1988

Unit 2.25

Source A: Simon Mason, *Social Problems 1760–914,* Basil Blackwell, 1986

Sources C & G: Quoted in Howard Martin, *Britain Since 1800: Towards the Welfare State*

Source D: Philip Sauvain, *British Economic and Social History*

Unit 2.26

Sources B & C: Howard Martin, *Britain Since 1800: Towards the Welfare State*

Source E: Simon Mason, *Social Problems 1760–1914*

Unit 2.27

Source A: Simon Mason, *Trade Unions and Social Change 1750–1980,* Basil Blackwell, 1987

Unit 2.28

Source A: J. Robottom, *A Social and Economic History of Industrial Britain*

Source B: Simon Mason, *Trade Unions and Social Change*

Unit 2.29

Sources B and C: Howard Martin, *Britain Since 1700: The Rise of Industry,* Macmillan Education, 1988

Source F: Simon Mason, *Trade Unions and Social Change*